101 WAYS TO ENJOY RETIREMENT ACROSS AMERICA

FIND NEW PASSIONS AND PURPOSE WITH CREATIVE
ACTIVITIES, PROJECTS, AND HOBBIES FROM ALL 50 STATES

RAVINA M CHANDRA

RMC PUBLISHERS

Copyright © 2022 by Ravina M Chandra

All rights reserved.

No part of this publication may be reproduced in any form or by any means, electronic or mechanical, including photocopying, recording, or any information browsing, storage, or retrieval system, without prior permission in writing from the publisher.

Under no circumstance will any blame or legal responsibility be held against the publisher, or author, for any damages, reparation, or monetary loss due to the information contained within this book. Either directly or indirectly. You are responsible for your own choices, actions, and results.

Please note the information contained within this document is for educational and entertainment purposes only. All effort has been executed to present accurate, up to date, and reliable, complete information. No warranties of any kind are declared or implied. Readers acknowledge that the author is not engaging in the rendering of legal, financial, medical, or professional advice. The content within this book has been derived from various sources. Please consult a licensed professional before attempting any techniques outlined in this book.

Published by RMC Publishers

ISBN 978-1-7782681-7-5 (Hardcover)

ISBN 978-1-7782681-6-8 (Paperback)

ISBN 978-1-7782681-5-1 (E-book)

www.ravinachandra.com

ALSO BY RAVINA M CHANDRA

In the *Inspired Retirement Living* Series

101 Ways to Enjoy Retirement
101 More Ways to Enjoy Retirement

Other books

The Art of Senior Dating
Longevity and Eating Habits
My Vibrant Life

YOUR FREE GIFT

I'd like to offer you a gift to say thank you for purchasing this book. Here is a booklet for creating your perfect Morning Routine for better productivity, lowering stress, and developing healthy habits.

In '4 Simple Steps to Create Your Perfect Morning Routine,' you will learn:

• What a **morning routine** is and why it is essential

• The secret of creating a morning routine using these **four components** that will **align with your core values**

• How a morning routine can elevate your life so that you may live **vibrantly**, no matter if you are a student, working, or retired

Go to www.RavinaChandra.com/books to get it NOW!

TABLE OF CONTENTS

Introduction   xi

NEW ENGLAND

1. CONNECTICUT   3
   - American Sign Language   3
   - Ham Radio   4

2. MAINE   5
   - Macramé   5
   - Short Stories   6

3. MASSACHUSETTS   8
   - Bell Ringing   8
   - Locksport   9

4. NEW HAMPSHIRE   11
   - Antique Restoration   11
   - Vegetable Carving   12

5. RHODE ISLAND   15
   - Clam digging   15
   - RV Camping   17

6. VERMONT   19
   - Fly Tying   19
   - Mazes and Meditation   21

MID-ATLANTIC

7. DELAWARE   25
   - Starting a Business   25
   - Learning to Code   26

8. MARYLAND   28
   - Mahjong   28
   - Paludariums   29

9. NEW JERSEY	32
Graffiti	32
Cryptograms	33
10. NEW YORK	35
Fantasy Sports	35
Making Ice Cream	37
11. NORTH CAROLINA	39
Quilting	39
Feeding Squirrels	40
12. PENNSYLVANIA	42
Time Capsules	42
Miniature Art	43
13. VIRGINIA	46
Hiking	46
Wicca	48

THE SOUTH

14. ALABAMA	53
Hot Air Ballooning	53
Natural Wonders	54
15. ARKANSAS	57
Amateur Lapidary	57
Natural Hot Springs or Sauna	58
16. FLORIDA	60
Drive-in Theaters	60
Group Fitness	61
17. GEORGIA	62
Butterfly Breeding	62
Plane Spotting	64
18. KENTUCKY	66
Song Writing	66
Social Media	68
19. LOUISIANA	70
Jazz Appreciation	70

Fusion Cuisine	71
20. MISSISSIPPI	75
Riverboat Cruising	75
Pottery	76
21. SOUTH CAROLINA	78
Sand Art	78
Carnivorous Plants	80
22. TENNESSEE	82
Country Music	82
Volunteering	83
23. WEST VIRGINIA	85
Traveling the 'World'	85
Blacksmithing	86

MIDWEST

24. ILLINOIS	91
Model Trains	91
Tarot Card Reading	93
25. INDIANA	94
Amateur Racing	94
Technology Free	96
26. IOWA	97
Electric Bikes	97
Architecture Appreciation	98
27. KANSAS	100
Kansas Style Barbeque	100
Potluck	101
28. MICHIGAN	103
Letter Writing	103
Collecting Vinyl	104
29. MINNESOTA	106
Standup Paddle Boarding	106
State Fairs	107

30. MISSOURI 109
   Fountains 109
   Tablescaping 110

31. NEBRASKA 112
   Non-Violent Hunting 112
   Beekeeping 113

32. NORTH DAKOTA 115
   Pet Rocks 115
   Iris Folding 116

33. OHIO 118
   Line-Dancing 118
   Self-Help 119

34. SOUTH DAKOTA 120
   Portraiture 120
   Indoor Winter Sports 121

35. WISCONSIN 123
   Tree Shaping 123
   Cheese Making 126

SOUTHWEST

36. ARIZONA 131
   Coin Shooting 131
   Online Learning 132

37. COLORADO 134
   Book-Binding 134
   Sport Shooting 135

38. NEW MEXICO 136
   Spotting UFOs 136
   Feeding Hummingbirds 137

39. OKLAHOMA 139
   Folk Music 139
   Musical Theater 140

40. TEXAS 142
   Skipping Stones 142

Leather Pyrography	143
41. UTAH	145
Stargazing	145
Tabletop Games	146

WEST COAST

42. ALASKA	151
Snowshoeing	151
Dog Training	153
43. CALIFORNIA	155
Acting as an Extra	155
Poetry Slams	156
44. HAWAII	158
Ukulele	158
Hula	159
45. IDAHO	161
Going Green	161
Laughing Clubs	163
46. MONTANA	164
Disc Golf	164
Drone Photography	165
47. NEVADA	167
Card Games	167
Magic Tricks	168
48. OREGON	171
Home-Brewing Kombucha	171
Kaleidoscopes	172
49. WASHINGTON	175
Farmers Markets	175
Digital Libraries	176
50. WYOMING	178
National Parks	178
Facial Hair Art	179

WASHINGTON D.C.	181
Wedding Officiating	181
Final Thoughts	183
Endnotes	189

INTRODUCTION

America may be the land of opportunity, but retirement is the time of opportunity.

Now is your chance; all those ideas in the back of your mind that have been stewing for years are just waiting to come out. Think about every time you've said, "I've always wanted to try...", "one day I'm going to...", or "when I'm not so busy, I'll...", now is your chance to make it happen!

But many of us don't know where to start. Faced with the reality of more free time, it can be a difficult challenge to transition to doing what you love, or even just figuring out what it is that you are truly passionate about, instead of doing what you have to do or are supposed to do.

How many of us nearing retirement have heard others say, or maybe even wondered, "but if I stop working, what would I do all day?"

There are obvious ideas, like spending your days reading, golfing, traveling, fishing, or gardening, but what if you're not passionate about those activities? And even if you enjoy those hobbies, what if you can't see them filling up the next few decades of your life?

This book aims to get you thinking about what you really want and give yourself a reason or two to get up in the morning with a smile on your face. Not every hobby in this book will be a good fit for you or something you can reproduce exactly, but the goal here is inspiration. Getting ideas, figuring out how to create something similar for yourself, or even having something spark a passion inside you that you didn't even know was there. There could also be someone in your life looking for ways to fill their days instead of wasting time surfing the internet. The ideas in this book could be just the thing they need to get out of their rut and back into a groove.

On our tour around the USA, we will visit each of the 50 states. We'll learn about a few unique hobbies you can find in each of them and maybe even get a bit of history and local flavor. Unfortunately, there are just too many amazing activities in America to cover every favorite local pastime. Instead, the focus will be on the more unique ones you may not have heard of or thought about before.

I would also like to apologize in advance if your state was put in the 'wrong' region; some states always disagree with where they belong, so please don't take it personally.

One more thing to mention before you delve into the pages of this book, as I know some of you are wondering why I missed an obvious hobby for your state. For every chapter of this book, thorough research and interviews took place to ensure proper representation of hobbies and states. And as you can appreciate, there was only room to describe two hobbies per state. If you would like to share with me a hobby that you would like to see in a future book, reach out to me at my direct email below with your idea.

ravina@ravinachandra.com

Let's get started.

NEW ENGLAND

CONNECTICUT

The hobbies in this state will help us stay connect-icut-ed in our retirement years.

AMERICAN SIGN LANGUAGE

American sign language (ASL) was formalized at the American School for the Deaf in West Hartford, Connecticut, during the early 19th century. While it has been an invaluable invention for the deaf community, why would you learn ASL if none of your close friends or family are deaf?

Learning another language is good for your brain, and the further removed that new language is from your native tongue, the larger the benefits. ASL is entirely different from the English language, more so than any other spoken language, and has also been shown to improve people's spatial awareness and the ability to interpret visual cues in body language.

ASL is also a way to connect with the deaf community, something you may never have been aware of. Think of it as being able to explore a new culture without traveling around the world.

Finally, there are some practical benefits too. If you and your partner learned ASL, you could send messages to each other in secret, in a quiet movie theater, or at a show. If you are ever in a noisy area and don't want to shout, you can use a few quick signs and not be inconvenienced. Learning ASL gives you one more tool in your communication arsenal, and while you can probably get by without it, who knows what uses and benefits you'll discover.

Most people can pick up the basics of ASL in less than 100 hours, but you will likely need some formal instruction to make any progress and become fluent.

HAM RADIO

The American Radio Relay League is the national association for amateur radio and is based in Connecticut. Before smartphones and internet chat rooms, amateur radio was a popular way of communicating with strangers across the country. Think of it as the internet before the internet, and it's still around today! Connect with people around the country, and see just how far your homemade radio signals can reach. Radio contesting is a form of competitive amateur radio, where teams see how many other amateur stations they can contact in a set period.

Now, not to discourage you, but you will have to study, learn technical skills, and pass an exam to become a licensed radio operator. It would be well advised to do some sleuthing around to see if there are any local clubs in your area that can help you get started.

MAINE

From macramé to the macabre, Maine is where traditions and creativity are expressed in many different and surprising ways.

MACRAMÉ

Some hobbies are timeless and remain popular, outlasting all fads and trends that come and go. Other hobbies fall in and out of fashion and are regularly resurrected back into the public consciousness before gradually receding in an ongoing cycle of popularity and obscurity. Macramé is the second kind.

You may remember this art of creating 'knot sculptures' from the 1960s and 1970s, or you may have seen some recent trends of macramé becoming popular in the 2020s, but consider this quote:

> "This kind of fancy work is not a novelty, except in the sense that when anything becomes so old as to be forgotten, its revival has all the effect of a first appearance" - from Sylvia's Book of Macramé Lace, **1882**.

Macramé has been going through cycles of popularity for hundreds of years, and it is thought that sailors staving off boredom by making hammocks, hats, and belts brought it to the USA.

You can start by finding some rope, twine, or yarn around the house and watching a few knotting tutorials online[1]; then, you can start creating. Common macramé projects include wall hangings, planters, key chains, belts, and hanging chairs or hammocks. You can add some style to your knots with beads or rings, and while it may seem simple at first, there are dozens of knots to master and plenty of room to grow and learn.

What's old is new again, so even if macramé falls out of fashion, you can be pretty sure it will be popular again if you wait long enough.

SHORT STORIES

Perhaps one of the most famous horror writers ever, Stephen King, was born in Maine and continues to live there today. Becoming a prolific author is a tall order for a hobby; King is also known for his work in short stories.

That seems more manageable, right? Instead of planning out hundreds of pages, subplots, and character arcs, all you need to string together is a few thousand words. Nobody starts learning music by trying to conduct an orchestra, or improving their fitness by running a marathon, so why would you begin writing with the pressure of a full-length novel?

Everyone has a story to tell, and probably at least a few. Even if they aren't epic literary feasts, sometimes all people are looking for is a bite-sized literary snack. So dust off your thesaurus, put away that self-consciousness, and try your hand at writing something you can be proud of.

There are several books, communities, and likely local groups or classes you could join to get support from other aspiring writers. And while you might not feel like a real writer if you set your sights on short stories, remember what one famous author said, "brevity is the soul of wit."

MASSACHUSETTS

We're going to go a little more traditional here and pick up some hobbies that need a bit of old-fashioned dexterity and coordination.

BELL RINGING

Have you ever been walking through a neighborhood on a Sunday morning and stopped to listen to the church bells ringing? While a large bell, or set of a dozen or more bells, seems like a normal part of an older church building or cathedral, did you ever wonder how all that sound gets made? Many people assume that church bells are automated now, either by a machine ringing the bells at the press of a button or maybe the sound is just a recording being played over a speaker. But to this day, in many buildings across America, the bells are played by a band of volunteer bell-ringers that are responsible for the Sunday morning music.

One of the oldest traditions of bell ringing is found at the Groton School in Massachusetts, a private Episcopal college where there has been a bell-ringing club active at the school's chapel since the early

1900s, with varying degrees of popularity (and annoyance from distracted students.)

The most popular form of bell-ringing is English full-circle ringing. The bells are situated in large circle rings within the belfry and attached by a rope to the room below, the ringing chamber. The bell-ringers pull down on the ropes and swing the bells like a pendulum in a circular frame. The ringers can control the speed of the bells, and with a lot of coordination and practice, they can play rounds or changes.

Rounds are when the bells are rung from the highest to lowest note in the sequence, which is also the lightest to the heaviest bells. This is a simple and familiar pattern that is easy to follow.

Changes are more complex patterns and are usually a series of rounds where the bells change their order in a pre-defined method, starting and ending with the original round going from high note to low note. Changes can become quite elaborate and require a lot of concentration to keep the bells playing in the correct order and some physical skill to manipulate how the bells swing. Many groups of bell-ringers regularly practice (with dampers on the bells) so that the Sunday ringing goes smoothly.

You don't necessarily have to be a church member; groups always look for new members to learn this specialized skill. And don't worry, no musical talent is necessary, but you do have to be able to count if your group is learning a complicated round!

LOCKSPORT

Many people spend their old age wishing they had been more rebellious during their younger years. Even though we're older and wiser, the pull of being a rebellious outlaw still has a strong place in American culture that never entirely goes away no matter how old you get.

While not many of us want to spend our golden years in a jail cell, the folks at the Massachusetts Institute of Technology may have a solution for you.

Locksport is the hobby of defeating security systems. This often involves lock-picking, and locksport groups will gather together and share tips, learn new techniques, and participate in contests. Organized locksport is a relatively new hobby, and the first groups began in Europe in the late 1990s.

Think of it as solving a tiny puzzle, with the pieces hidden away in a metal case to obscure your vision, that gives off a supremely satisfying 'click' when solved.

There are cheap and easy locks to start with, and as your skill increases, you can progress to more difficult ones. There is always something interesting to work towards and a never-ending source of new challenges for your mind and fingers. If you feel up for it, you can enter a locksport competition and try your skills against others.

The best place to start learning this hobby is the MIT Guide to Lock Picking[1], which explains how locks work and the basics of lock-picking techniques.

Now I know what you're thinking. This sounds illegal, or at least unethical, and seems like a great way to get into some serious trouble. But the philosophy behind locksport might help ease your conscience. The core tenants of locksport are full disclosure and promoting improvements in physical security. Full disclosure means that your new hobbies are all done in the open, with the approval of the lock owners, and never on private property. The locksport community also discloses any strategies and techniques to the lock manufacturers so that they can improve their locks in the future or help consumers learn how to keep themselves more secure.

NEW HAMPSHIRE

The hobbies of New Hampshire are about turning the common into the extraordinary and giving new life to things of old, a fitting premise for a state where the constitution was ratified, and the new country of America was born.

ANTIQUE RESTORATION

Why not make something old, new again? I'm not talking about spending more time in the gym or getting some cosmetic surgery; this is much easier.

Collecting and restoring antiques is a popular hobby throughout the US, but nowhere more so than in New Hampshire. New England's famous antique alley starts in Portsmouth, New Hampshire, and over its distance, travels past 500+ antique shops. You can find almost anything here, which is why antique restoration is a great hobby.

You can take almost any object you have some interest in and begin finding antique versions. Restoring antiques doesn't have to be complicated or take a workshop full of power tools. While popular items like furniture, cars, or paintings might be a challenge (or expensive), there are many simple things to restore. Instead of just collecting items to put on a shelf, take things a step further and attempt to restore them to their former glory.

Here are some examples of inexpensive, easy-to-find, and easy-to-restore items that could make great hobbies:

- Cast iron cookware - a little bit of elbow grease and baking soda can make an ancient cast iron pan look new again
- Vintage jeans and clothing - a sewing machine or hand stitch might be all you need, or if your fingers aren't as nimble, you could try adding patches
- Belt buckles - these or any other small metal objects or collectibles can often be given new life with a dash of metal polish
- Costume jewelry - may take a little more dedication and creativity to restore, but you'll end up with pieces and styles nobody else can find
- Glass - mirrors or glassware can be given new life with a vinegar solution and a mild abrasive (uncooked rice can work)

VEGETABLE CARVING

Keene, New Hampshire, is the pumpkin carving capital of the world and holds the record for most lit jack-o'-lanterns in one place[1]. But carving vegetables doesn't have to be limited to a Halloween activity.

Many people would like to try carving or creating sculptures, but the first (and biggest) hurdles are finding the space, tools, and raw materials to work with. Unfortunately, not all of us have a dedicated woodworking workshop or access to marble slabs to begin learning the art of sculpture. So here are some examples of vegetable carving that could be practiced before you move on to more permanent forms or just a way to enhance the presentation of a meal with a decorative centerpiece.

Flowers are a common theme, but portraits, scenes, and other imaginative options are possible. You can easily get started with a set of standard sharpened kitchen knives, but as with most hobbies, you can invest in some more advanced tools. For example, fruit and vegetable carving sets are made of smaller knives with impressively curved shapes, strangely patterned blades, and elaborate peelers. These will allow you to go all in here and get wild with your creations.

So if you're looking at getting into sculpture but would appreciate a way to erase any mistakes with a midnight snack, this could be the hobby for you.

Basic edible flowers made with pumpkin[2]

Advanced edible flower arrangement from a wide variety of fruits[3]

RHODE ISLAND

The Ocean State is unique amongst the original 13 colonies, founded by a refugee fleeing religious persecution[1]. From this beginning, Rhode Island has become a state known for free-thinking and independence, and those characteristics will serve you well if you decide to pursue the following two hobbies.

CLAM DIGGING

If you are near a beach and own a spade, trowel, or hoe and a bucket, you can dig yourself up a nice dinner. While residents of Rhode Island can go out and harvest shellfish recreationally, if you're a tourist or living in another state, you might need a license similar to a hunting license. Don't let that minor setback deter you; there is nothing more satisfying than a dinner you dug up yourself!

Clam season is relatively long, often extending through the entire winter from September to May. A typical clam dig lasts only about an hour before low tide, but that's plenty of time to harvest enough clams to use over the next day.

Depending on where you live, you might be able to find clams, mussels, oysters, or scallops. Most can be found by looking for small depressions in the sand at low tide, then pounding or thumping the ground next to it. If water squirts out, dig a hole about 7 or 8 inches deep, and you should find a clam for your bucket (you might have to rake through your excavation as sometimes, they are hard to spot.) Don't forget to refill your hole and leave the beach precisely the way you found it.

Check for any closures or warnings due to safety or pollution concerns. If any shellfish you harvest smells off (they should smell like the ocean,) or if they don't look bright and clean, don't take the risk and just put them back. Shellfish can accumulate disease-causing pathogens, and the local health department will usually do regular testing to ensure shellfish are safe to eat.

As a bit of inspiration, here is a recipe for clam chowder[2].

Ingredients

- 4 dozen small clams, cleaned and scrubbed
- 4 thick slices of bacon, chopped
- 1 large onion, diced
- salt
- 1 1/2 pounds of potatoes, diced (½ inch)
- 3 tablespoons of flour
- 2 cups heavy cream
- thyme
- bay leaves
- olive oil

Directions

- Place the clams and 1 cup of water in a large pot. Cover and place over high heat and cook the clams for 6 to 7 minutes. Uncover and remove the open clams. Cover the pot again and

continue cooking the clams that haven't opened yet. Cook the clams for another 2 to 3 minutes. Turn off the heat and discard any clams that have not opened. Strain the liquid from the pot through a mesh strainer lined with a coffee filter and save it for later.
- Coarsely chop the clams.
- Drizzle a few drops of olive oil into the bottom of the clam pot and toss in the bacon. Bring the pan to medium heat. When the bacon has become brown and crispy, toss in the onions and season lightly with salt. Cook the onions until they are very soft and aromatic but have no color, 7 to 8 minutes. Add the potatoes and cook for another 5 minutes.
- Sprinkle the flour over the onions and potato mixture and stir to combine. Gradually whisk in the clam juice. When the clam juice has been whisked in, and there are no lumps, whisk in the cream and toss in some bay leaves and thyme. Taste for seasoning and adjust if needed. Bring to a boil and reduce to a simmer until the potatoes are cooked for 10 to 15 minutes.
- Toss in the clams. Taste and add more seasoning if needed.

RV CAMPING

Just getting out and seeing the entirety of the United States is a lifetime hobby all on its own, and the best way to do that is on the open road. If you fly between the big cities, you'll miss out on many all-American flavors. So instead, just like Rhode Island is a tiny state, you can take a tiny home with you and use your RV to take in as much of the USA as possible.

There is no set rule for what is considered an RV other than being a recreational vehicle. It could range anywhere from a converted VW bus to a 40-foot motorhome. It depends on your budget, how much space you need to feel comfortable, and what luxuries you can't live without. Whether you need a tent under the stars or prefer to be glamping in style, with a bit of planning, anyone can come up with a way to enjoy the journey and the destination.

Over 10,000 RV parks in the US and over 1,000 state parks can accommodate RVs. That's a lot of weekends away!

So, where should you start? Here are some of the most famous American road trips:

- Let's start in Rhode Island, traveling through New England in the fall and passing through Maine, New Hampshire, Vermont, Massachusetts, and Connecticut
- Route 66 from Santa Monica to Chicago, make sure to give yourself at least three weeks
- The Blues Highway around the Florida panhandle and the Gulf of Mexico, ending in New Orleans
- Or, for something more scenic, try the Oregon Coast Highway 101

So pull out those old paper maps, or get your smartphone to give you directions, and get out there and see your country with your own eyes.

VERMONT

We're going back to some relaxing hobbies in Vermont. Rushing around trying to fit in every possible activity will wear you out, so here are a few quiet, introspective hobbies to consider.

FLY TYING

Fishing is one of those 'common' retirement hobbies people seem to gravitate to. Along with golf, gardening, and reading, fishing can be a great hobby but isn't unique.

But an excellent way to turn a run-of-the-mill, ordinary hobby into a unique hobby is to specialize. Find that one aspect that speaks to you and go all-in on that. Maybe you don't even find the hobby as a whole all that intriguing, but you seem drawn to that one part.

Fly tying could be just the thing for you.

Fly tying, or fly dressing, is the art of crafting the artificial flies used as bait by fly fishing anglers. You don't need much space, a small workbench or table will do, and only a few tools:

- A small vise or clamp to hold the hook
- A bobbin to keep the thread tight and to hold it for you
- Gauges and pliers to measure the hook size and to hold the fly when wrapping it
- Hair stackers, tubes used to align the fly's 'hairs' before tying them on
- Scissors and tweezers for cutting and grabbing, and
- A whip finisher to tie a thread around the hook.

The Fly Dresser's Workbench[1]

The materials used to make the fly are also easy to find. Hooks, thread, feathers, and beads are common fly tying ingredients usually available at local craft stores.

So find yourself a bench, set up your workstation (a magnifying glass will also come in handy to get those fine details,) and research some local fly's to practice tying. Most common flies have fly patterns, or 'recipes,' which describe what materials you need and how to tie them. Thousands of fly patterns are available with a bit of searching on the internet or at the library.

This hobby could either enhance your everyday fishing experience into something unique, or maybe you could start a collection of your favorite-looking fly replicas.

MAZES AND MEDITATION

Sometimes the best way to relax and clear your mind is to get lost. And where is the best place to get yourself lost? Why a maze, of course!

The Great Vermont Corn Maze is the largest maze in New England. It takes over two hours to get through but don't get intimidated; you can leave at any time through an emergency exit and take a break. There is no comparison between trying to solve a paper maze on a page compared to being 'immersed' in a physical maze. It activates your brain differently and gets those gray cells firing.

But you probably don't have access to a wide variety of corn mazes near your home. So, what other types of physical mazes can you find?

Labyrinth meditation involves walking along a set pattern, calming your mind. These paths are usually laid out in stones or tiles on the ground and are commonly found around churches or cathedrals, representing mini-pilgrimages. They fold in and around themselves, often taking up no more than a few yards of space, with the end visible or right next to the start and your own discipline being the only thing holding you to the path.

Of course, you won't get physically stuck or lost in these mazes, but spending 10 to 15 minutes walking the labyrinth pattern is a great way to get yourself mentally unstuck.

22 | 101 WAYS TO ENJOY RETIREMENT ACROSS AMERICA

Labyrinth on floor of Grace Cathedral, San Francisco[2]

MID-ATLANTIC

DELAWARE

The hobbies of Delaware are serious business, but that doesn't mean they can't also be fun.

STARTING A BUSINESS

You've retired from work; I get that. So why would you want to head back into the daily grind and start over? But things are different now. You don't have to slave away working for somebody else or toil at a job that isn't fulfilling; you can be your own boss, work on things meaningful to you, and even better, you don't have to prove anything to anybody except maybe yourself.

Due to some very business-friendly tax laws, Delaware is the business capital of the USA. Almost half of all American corporations are based in Delaware, and there might not be any better place to start a new company or get that dream idea off the ground.

There are also so many more options available today than in the past. Maybe you had a dynamite idea ahead of its time, and the world has finally caught up to it.

New computer-based tools also mean that stressful parts of business like accounting, logistics, and other specialties requiring hiring staff can now be automated or outsourced. Starting a new project has never been easier, and there are countless resources available to get you started. All you need is that million-dollar idea.

If money isn't a big motivator anymore, maybe a non-profit or charitable organization would be more your style. Whatever you choose, put those years of experience and knowledge to use, but this time directed at the goals that make you happy and continue to give you purpose long into your golden years. It's never too late to leave your mark or make a difference.

LEARNING TO CODE

As we get older, many of us reach a point where we no longer want to keep up with technology. You might think, 'leave it to the kids (or grandkids) to figure that all out,' or 'I'm too old to learn how to use that new smartphone.' And while you can definitely get by without all the latest gadgets, being technologically illiterate is starting to become a significant handicap in daily life. What if you couldn't access your bank, book a trip, or keep in touch with family? Even if you have enough know-how to use the internet and technology of today, will you be able to keep it up into your twilight years?

One of the best ways to ensure you don't end up reliant on others is to have a solid understanding of the basics. So while learning the ins and outs of the latest tech news might not be appealing, if you understand the general ideas of how these things work, you'll be well suited to take on the future.

So why not try coding and learn how to speak to your machines.

Just like learning a new language, all it takes is practice (and probably a book or two from the library.) One of the easiest and most popular coding languages to learn is called Python[1], and the Python Software

Foundation has its headquarters in Delaware. Python is a good choice for beginners, as it's easy to read and structured just like the English language.

Whether you create the next big app, gain insight into why your computer is acting up, or keep your mind active learning something new, this hobby will keep you firmly planted in the digital age. The opportunities and different angles you can explore with coding are endless and only limited by your imagination.

MARYLAND

The people of Maryland have adapted some hobbies originally from other countries and put their own personal spin on them, something worth trying for yourself.

MAHJONG

Just because something didn't originate in America doesn't mean it can't be an American hobby. Mahjong, a tile-based game for up to four people from China, has become popular in the US in recent years. In fact, a variant, aptly called American-Mahjong, was created by the American Mah-jongg Association, based out of Baltimore.

There are many variations in the rules and tiles, but here is the general idea of how a mahjong game is played.

A set of 144 tiles is used. These can be divided into three suits (dots, bamboo, and characters) numbered from 1 to 9, along with honor tiles (4 wind tiles and 3 dragon tiles) and two sets of 4 bonus tiles (representing flowers and seasons). The bonus tiles also have a direction associated with them (north, south, east, or west) which gives a player bonus points if they are seated in that same direction at the table.

A mahjong game has four rounds, each representing one of the cardinal directions, and always starts with the east, then goes to the south, west, and finishing to the north. Each round has at least four hands, with each player acting as the dealer (in the east position) once.

Instead of changing seats around the table, a 'wind marker' is used to show which seat is in the eastern 'dealer' spot for each hand. If the dealer wins the hand or is a draw, an extra hand is played with the same positions.

At the start of each hand, the tiles are placed face down, and the players each choose 36 tiles and arrange them in two rows of 18. The next step varies based on house rules, but each player is randomly given a hand of 13 tiles.

The game begins in earnest, and each player selects a new tile to add to their hand and then discards a tile (either the one they drew or one from their hand). Flowers and seasons are not counted as part of a hand and are set aside for bonus points, and another tile is drawn. Play continues until one player creates a winning hand of 14 tiles and calls out mahjong!

Winning hands are made up of only groups of tiles. These groups, or melds, can be groups of two, three, or four identical tiles or three or more tiles, all of the same suit in numerical sequence.

This is similar to many run-based card games, so if you are familiar with those, you can pick mahjong up quickly.

PALUDARIUMS

What the heck is a paludarium? It combines a terrarium and an aquarium, incorporating plants (and sometimes animals) that live underwater and/or on land. They usually aim to recreate environments like swamps, bogs, marshes, or wetlands.

Terrariums were started by the English in the 1800s (then known as Wardian cases) and were used to study plants and transport local fauna to the colonies. Aquascaping, the art of underwater gardening, is a hobby that originates in Japanese and Dutch cultures, each with its own style. The Dutch style is well-ordered and manicured, while the Japanese style is focused on creating picturesque landscapes. Paludariums combine these two types into one.

Although this hobby and the individual hobbies of keeping terrariums and aquariums are widespread across the USA, the winner of the first Aquatic Gardeners Association competition in 2000 was an entry from Cockeysville, Maryland.

Tropical paludarium[1]

Paludariums are usually built in aquarium tanks or enclosed (waterproof) cases and can come in almost any size or shape. After deciding on the type of environment you want to create, you first add the terrestrial (land) elements; then, once those are established, you can fill in the aquatic (water) based ones. This hobby can take a bit of research. Many beginners might start with either a terrarium or aquarium on their own first and focus on creating thriving plant life instead of adding any animals.

NEW JERSEY

New Jersey has attitude; there is no other way to say it. The two hobbies here reflect the proud, in-your-face personality New Jersey is known for, as well as their sometimes difficult-to-understand accent.

GRAFFITI

Street art has slowly made its way into museums, transitioning from the underground art scene of New Jersey to high-end auction houses. Marc Ecko, a New Jersey-born graffiti artist, also transitioned from the streets and became a famous fashion designer. But New Jersey remains a lesser-known hotspot for graffiti and public murals to this day.

Now, sneaking out in the middle of the night with some spray cans and stencils might be good for a thrill, but there are other (legal) ways to make your mark. Many public spaces and buildings encourage community artwork and public participation. Often relying on the work of volunteers or community groups, who knows, there might be a chance to spray paint a building near you! Brightening up your community and giving tired old streets some personality can brighten up anyone's day, regardless of artistic tastes. If you're not having luck finding a place for some 'free' artwork near you, try searching at http://www.legal-walls.net/.

Before you get out there and start tagging your local grocer (that politely requested some color to spice up the exterior of their old shop,) here are some basics for spray paint graffiti, straight from 1970s New Jersey:

- Remember to shake the can well before using; the paint needs to be mixed
- Thin coats of paint are much less likely to drip, so stand back, take your time and use multiple thin coats instead of giving the wall a close-range blast, and don't spray any one spot for too long; keep that can moving
- Stand closer and move faster for thin lines, and stand further away to make thick ones; controlling how far you are from the wall is important
- Be careful when you press that nozzle; starting too early or holding on too long can make things look messy
- Don't write over others' hard work
- Remember to add your own personal tag
- And of course, the only way to get better is to practice!

CRYPTOGRAMS

Doing the daily crossword or sudoku puzzle might help keep your mind sharp, but there is a whole world of exciting and challenging ways to test your brain. After all, doing the same mental exercise only trains your brain for that one activity; why not branch out into some lesser-known brain-teasers. We can take some inspiration here from Bell Labs, located in Murray Hill, New Jersey, home to some of America's best minds in cryptography, or code-breaking, one of the most challenging puzzles.

Cryptograms, also called ciphers, have been around for millennia. The most straightforward kinds involve replacing each individual letter in a message with a different one. Called a monoalphabetic substitution cipher, this scrambles up each word fairly well but in a consistent pattern in which a little sleuthing and logic can crack pretty reliably with little practice. A similar cipher, called a Caesar cipher, shifts each letter of the alphabet by a set number of letters. Cipher puzzles can be made more difficult by giving fewer clues, removing details like punctuation or word spacing, or being shorter and providing less information to the solver.

More difficult cryptograms might rely on a code word that needs to be solved, guessed, or deduced to help decode the rest of the puzzle. These can also be combined with other puzzles like crosswords or anagrams to become more and more difficult as you refine your code-breaking skills.

Luckily it's easy to find a wide variety of these puzzles in newspapers, websites, and books. And if you ever get bored solving them, you can always try your hand at creating your very own devilish cipher to hide your secrets in plain sight.

NEW YORK

You could probably come up with 101 hobbies just for the state of New York. Let's start with these two great ways to enjoy a Sunday or a sundae.

FANTASY SPORTS

While I'm not going to condone that you start gambling away your pension on football games, this is a way to make watching sports a little more interesting and require a little more brain power. You may have always dreamed of having the time to follow your favorite team and watch all of their games, but that's probably not doing much to keep you mentally or physically sharp.

So while this hobby won't do much for the physical side of things, fantasy sports can help keep your brain engaged and make spectating a little more active for your gray matter.

There are online and offline fantasy sports leagues everywhere, with slightly different rules and variations, but before we get into the details, how about a brief history lesson. The first modern version of fantasy sports was a baseball league started by sports journalists in New York.

It was based on previous versions that used baseball cards. But this new version used statistics from the current season instead of players' historical performance (detailed on the backs of those cards) to simulate games. This added a degree of unpredictability to the mix and made the outcome of the league dependent on what was happening during the 'real' season.

For those unfamiliar, here is how it works. At the beginning of the season, fantasy league members undertake a 'fantasy draft' and pick players for their 'fantasy team.' This is typically done in a per-round style, with each member getting to select one player per round. Some rounds may have pre-defined restrictions or requirements, like no-pitchers or rookies only.

Once each league member has selected an entire team, statistics can be collected once the season starts. Points are awarded (and occasionally deducted) for each player's performance, for example, hits, stolen bases, home runs, or strikeouts. Every player on the members' fantasy team contributes to their overall score, even though they will all be playing on different teams and in different games in the actual league.

This can mean that instead of cheering for one team, someone involved in fantasy sports might be cheering for a dozen or more players spread across multiple teams, giving more games more meaning.

At the end of the season, all of the players' points each time are tallied up. While this used to be done by hand, these days, there is a lot of software that does the tracking and scoring for you, so your league won't need its own secretary and statistician. Whoever has the most points wins the season!

There are fantasy sports leagues for most popular sports, with varying degrees of seriousness. Find something that fits your personality, and you'll quickly realize how complicated and mentally demanding managing a fantasy team can be.

MAKING ICE CREAM

Learning to cook can be an easy way to improve your diet, get healthier, and save money. A valuable life skill that can serve you well for years, teaching you discipline, organization, and cleanliness. Or you could skip right to the fun part and learn to make ice cream.

And where better to get inspiration than from the city of New York, where the first ice cream parlor opened up in 1790! In fact, records show that George Washington was such a fan of the new fad that he racked up a $200 bill at an ice cream parlor that summer[1].

Across America today, almost 10% of dairy production goes towards making ice cream, making it one of the most popular foods in the country[2].

There are countless varieties of ice cream across America and around the globe, from gelato to sorbet, frozen yogurt, or even an old-fashioned American banana split. So you'll be able to find your own favorite signature style and make it as healthy (or unhealthy) as you wish.

Learning to perfect a single type of food, whether ice cream is your choice or something else, is a great way to make cooking into a more interesting hobby.

Here is an easy ice cream recipe that doesn't need an ice cream maker to get you started. You can experiment with this and use it as a foundation to create your own masterpiece.

Ingredients

- Heavy whipping cream
- Sweetened condensed milk

Directions

- Whip the heavy cream until stiff peaks form

- Fold the whipped cream into the sweetened condensed milk
- You can take a detour here and add any additional flavors, like vanilla extract
- Gently pour the mixture into an 8×5-inch pan (a metal will freeze the ice cream faster)
- Freeze for a few hours and serve! You might have to let the ice cream sit for a few minutes at room temperature before scooping

NORTH CAROLINA

Let's take it easy and look into some relaxing hobbies for North Carolina. These might feel like typical 'old-person' hobbies, but we'll put a unique North Carolinian spin on them.

QUILTING

Gwendolyn Ann Magee, from High Point in North Carolina, only learned to quilt after her daughters enrolled in college. Even though she entered the art world later in life, she made a tremendous impact as a 'fiber artist.' She was a pioneer in depicting African American history and culture through her quilts and became known for bold political statements.

So no matter how old-fashioned or out-of-style you think an art form or hobby seems, maybe all it needs to get some new life is your unique perspective. Many of America's diverse regions and cultures have distinctive quilting styles, from the floral designs with handwritten accents of Baltimore quilts to the irregular geometric patterns of 'crazy' quilts, Native American star quilts, or story-telling style African American quilts. Maybe you want to add a more exotic flair and look into styles from Europe, Asia, or Africa; almost every culture has come up with its unique style of quilting.

The basics of quilting are simple, and the primary skill you need is to be able to sew two pieces of fabric together. There are, of course, more advanced techniques and styles to learn, and as you advance in the hobby, you can make more elaborate and refined designs.

Another side of quilting is, of course, the quilting bee, where a group of women (but why not some men too) get together to work on a communal quilt. When was the last time you did a group art project? Was it back in grade school? An excuse to get together and catch up with friends and you are left with a beautiful, meaningful, and useful piece of artwork to share. Even if quilting is not your style, there are many communal projects you could find for your social group to change things up and keep life interesting.

FEEDING SQUIRRELS

The Eastern Gray squirrel is the official state mammal of North Carolina, and while it may not be the most exciting choice to represent your state, you can find these curious animals almost everywhere.

Feeding squirrels can be as simple as leaving out a few nuts on a railing, but if you do something, you may as well commit to it and give it your total effort. Here are some examples of overly elaborate, borderline ridiculous squirrel feeders. While you can always order one of these from a store, why not instead use these as inspiration to create your own feeder or obstacle course for the squirrels who live around you.

Windmills, slinkys, or ladders

Make getting those nuts a bit of a challenge by giving your feeder some moving parts.

Squirrel-sized chairs, benches, and picnic tables

A relaxing place to sit and get a cute picture taken.[1]

PENNSYLVANIA

In the state of Pennsylvania, considered by many to be the birthplace of our nation, we will learn how to make a significant impact using only small items.

TIME CAPSULES

Many of us probably remember filling and burying a time capsule sometime during our school years. Maybe it was planned to be opened after a year, decade, or even century. Still, it is always an interesting process to figure out how to capture a period of time and preserve it for future generations.

One of the world's first-time capsules was the 'Century Safe,' which was sealed in 1879 at the US Centennial Exposition in Philadelphia. The safe contained a gold pen and inkstand, a book on temperance, a collection of Americans' signatures, and snapshots of President Ulysses S. Grant[1]. While it was briefly lost during that period, it was rediscovered just in time for its scheduled opening at America's bicentennial celebration in July 1976.

While creating something for the historical record might be a little grand for most of us, there are plenty of other ways to leave behind memories, either for your future self or future generations. Here are a few ideas:

- Relationship time capsule - for mementos of your time with a significant other
- Baby or grandchild time capsule - to be opened on their 18th birthday
- Life's journey - to record memorable moments of your life for your children or grandchildren
- Special events - include items from a special occasion, trip, or achievement so you can celebrate again in the future

Time capsules aren't just for the people opening them in the future; they also force the capsule creators to think about what items best reflect the moment in time they are trying to capture. Think of it like journaling, where the act of writing something down helps you reflect on its importance, except instead of writing; you are selecting meaningful items. Creating time capsules is a great way to show your creativity and leave some lasting memories for the future.

MINIATURE ART

Painting is a common way for aspiring creators to dip their toes into the world of art. Lessons can be taken at the local community center or online, supplies are available at nearby stores, and everyone remembers how much fun it was to have an art class back in school. But miniature art may be the thing if you're looking for something a little bit different.

Most of the best-known American miniature painters are women. Pioneers like Karen Latham and her daughters, Narcissa Niblack

Thorne and Margaret Hicks, aren't household names but are known throughout the art world. Born in Pennsylvania, Margaret Hicks was a leader in miniature art, including paintings (often less than 4 inches in size), engravings, and sculptures.

Hamilton Pool, a 2.5" by 3.5" oil painting[2]

An easy way to get into miniature painting is to start with matchbook or matchbox art. Using a matchbox as a canvas, all you need is a fine detail paintbrush and a magnifying glass. This artform is becoming quite popular online, and you can find numerous examples of miniature matchbox art online to give you some ideas. Choose whatever subject matter or style speaks to you.

As an added benefit, you save money on expensive canvases and paints; it's much easier to store and display your minute masterpieces.

"There is something fascinating about the exquisite art of miniature painting. The skill of the artist, reflected in the detail and delicate quality of the painting, reveals a world view often overlooked, except by those who take the time to see." — Margaret Hicks

VIRGINIA

C onnecting with nature, physically or spiritually, is the focus of the hobbies in Virginia.

HIKING

Many people enjoy a brisk stroll in the morning to get their blood flowing. Walking may be an underrated form of exercise, but it is probably a bit of a stretch to call your morning circuit around the block a hobby. On the other hand, the Appalachian Trail is the longest hiking trail in the world, covering 2,200 miles and passing through 14 states, including Virginia. Hiking trails like the Appalachian would be considered an impressive hobby.

Don't worry if you're getting up there in years; you can always go at your own pace; after all, people have completed the entire Appalachian Trail in their eighties[1].

In everyday language, hiking is a pretty general term. If you're going for a hike, you're headed out for a longish walk in nature, usually on an outdoor trail that is probably a bit rough but relatively safe and not too strenuous. But as with any hobby, those serious about it have developed their specific vocabulary, describing a wide range of options and experiences. For example, if a hike has some steep sections that require using your hands, that is called 'scrambling.' Some hikes might be steep and require some climbing, but they will specify whether the climb is roped (using climbing gear and safety equipment) or unroped (short, manageable sections that beginners can handle.) Additional equipment, like trekking poles, can make things easier and improve stability. The most popular hiking areas have multiple routes at different levels of challenge. Using the Swiss SAC hiking scale[2], here are some examples of hike difficulty classifications:

T1 Hiking: Paths are well marked and secured, the terrain is flat or slightly inclined, and there is no danger of falling. These can be walked in regular footwear.

T2 Mountain Hiking: Paths are marked, but there may be steep sections with danger of falling. Specific hiking footwear and some basic navigation skills are recommended.

T3 Challenging Mountain Hiking: There are usually footpaths, but there may be sections secured with ropes and chains and steep pathless terrain with some danger of falling. Good hiking shoes and steady footing are a requirement, along with some basic alpine experience.

T4 Alpine Walking: There won't necessarily be paths, and you might need to use your hands to scramble. They require some experience and very stable trekking shoes and should not be undertaken by beginners.

T5 Challenging Alpine Walking: There usually won't be a path, and there may be some simple climbing sections, steep rocky slopes, and danger of slips and falls. These require mountaineering boots, the ability to assess alpine terrain, and good navigation skills. Knowing how to handle a rope is also recommended.

T6 Difficult Alpine Walking: These are primarily unmarked and without paths, with tricky rocky slopes and some climbing sections.

Experts only, you'll need proper equipment and experience to take these on.

So don't worry if you have no desire to go on a T6 expedition; there is plenty of fun to be had at T1 and T2; make sure you are adequately prepared, have your map handy, and set out for adventure!

WICCA

Colonial America has a storied history of witchcraft, false allegations, and unjust persecution that lasted in Virginia until the 1700s. As a result, a modern, nature-based, pagan movement called Wicca is often confused with witchcraft. Wicca has been increasing in popularity since the beginning of the movement in the 1940s and continues to grow today. The number of self-identified Wiccans in America grew from 8,000 in 1990 to 342,000 in 2008[3].

So why would you choose to take up Wicca in retirement?

- Their moral code is (loosely translated) 'if it harms none, do what you will'
- Wicca has life-affirming principles and seeks to minimize harm to oneself and others
- The Law of Threefold Return is similar to the concept of Karma, except your good (and bad) actions are returned to you threefold
- Wiccans seek to achieve the eight virtues: mirth, reverence, honor, humility, strength, beauty, power, and compassion

If you are not a religious person by nature or upbringing, adopting a spiritual practice can give you some purpose and direction and help build a social community in retirement.

Wicca is a popular option, but there are several similar movements that might fit your beliefs and lifestyle better. Take a look around; joining something larger than yourself might be just what you need after finishing your career or starting the next chapter in your life.

THE SOUTH

ALABAMA

The hobbies of Alabama will inspire you to see the world around you from a different perspective.

HOT AIR BALLOONING

An annual event every Memorial Day weekend since 1978, the Alabama Jubilee Hot-Air Balloon Classic is one of the oldest balloon races in the USA. It has grown to include 60 balloons representing over 20 states[1].

Hot-air balloons have been around since the late 1700s and are a much more relaxed way to fly than planes. Floating above the land in a relaxing hot-air balloon ride might seem more like a one-off adventure, but many have made it a full-time hobby.

While you do need a lighter-than-air pilot certificate from the FAA to fly your own balloon, there is no shortage of balloon operators willing to take you and some friends up in the air for a birds-eye tour. This is a great way to see a new destination and get your bearings or gain some appreciation for your favorite places.

Typically balloon rides start early in the morning, often before sunrise. Make sure to show up early so you can watch the whole process of the balloon being inflated and prepped for takeoff. Then you're into the basket and up in the air before you know it.

While balloons are somewhat at the mercy of local weather conditions, your pilot will probably be able to land you at least fairly close to where you started. Many balloon rides end with a picnic and a champagne toast, and they are a great way to spend a morning and afternoon.

If you happen to have a fear of heights, maybe your hobby could just be attending hot-air balloon festivals or making your own small-scale balloons.

On the other hand, if you find floating through the sky to be something you enjoy, you could branch out into something more adventurous like paragliding. Just make sure to be careful on those landings!

NATURAL WONDERS

What is a natural wonder? There is no strict definition, but Alabama has some great examples of places representing unique natural conditions that most people never get to see.

Things that happen in nature so rarely, are worth a trip off the beaten path, and since America is so large and diverse, you could easily spend your later decades traveling around to seek these magical locations out.

A natural bridge, or natural arch, is a rock formation formed by thousands of years of erosion. One of the largest natural bridges is found in Alabama and can only be appreciated in person. Similarly, many of America's natural wonders must be seen to be believed.

A natural arch[2]

Here are a few other examples of natural wonders that are worth seeking out:

- The Wave in Arizona. A sandstone rock formation with colorful swirling patterns is a favorite of photographers.
- Niagara Falls in New York. While some may argue that the Canadian side of the falls is more impressive, all three of the waterfalls here (Horseshoe Falls, American Falls, and Bridal Veil Falls) would be a destination on their own.
- Jug Rock in Indiana. A freestanding rock formation shaped like a table, the largest of its kind in the eastern United States.
- Crater Lake in Oregon. Formed by a collapsed volcano, this nearly 2,000-foot-deep lake is known for its vibrant blue shade and is one of America's most pristine water bodies.

- Mendenhall Ice Caves in Alaska. Bright blue ice caves formed off the edge of a receding glacier; you probably will want a guide to ensure you have a safe trip.
- Lava flows in Hawaii. Seeing cooled lava flows in person in the Hawaiian Islands.
- Balanced Rock in Utah. A massive boulder precariously balanced on a stone spire 70 feet off the ground.
- Hamilton Pool in Texas. A stunning jade green pool formed by the collapse of an underground river.
- Great Sand Dunes in Colorado. You don't have to visit the Sahara to see giant dunes; the ones in this national park can reach 750 feet tall.

ARKANSAS

The hobbies from Arkansas have a geological twist, well-fitting the state, which is home to the outstanding Ozark and Ouachita mountains.

AMATEUR LAPIDARY

Lapidary is the art of shaping stones, minerals, or gems into decorative items. There are many different skills used in lapidary. While cutting facets into a diamond isn't necessarily the most attainable hobby, some basic lapidary skills like rock tumbling are accessible to any amateur. Speaking of diamonds, the state gem of Arkansas is the diamond, the most famous of all the precious stones.

So what exactly is rock tumbling, and what do you need to start?

A rock tumbler is a reasonably small machine consisting of a continuously rotated motorized barrel. You fill it with rocks, and as they bounce and crash against each other along with some coarse grit, they become smoother, with the rock tumbler acting similarly to how rocks would be thrown around in a river.

The process takes a few weeks, and as the stones get smoother, more refined and finer polishing agents are added. In the end, you have a collection of impressive-looking 'gems' that can be used for jewelry, decoration, or other imaginative art projects.

While any rock can be tumbled, dense minerals like quartz, agate, or jasper are the best. They look entirely different after polishing, so you might have to put on your amateur geologist hat to figure out where to find interesting stones and what they usually look like before being tumbled. To start, any rock that is hard, dense, solid without cracks or fractures, and relatively smooth is a good choice.

If you can see any color in the unpolished rock, remember that this will become much more vibrant and impressive after tumbling, so it's usually worth experimenting.

The satisfaction of finding the stones yourself, polishing them for a few weeks, then creating your own works of art can be extremely rewarding. Anyone who has ever wanted to create their own jewels, gems, or collection of minerals should give this a try.

NATURAL HOT SPRINGS OR SAUNA

Hot Springs National Park in Arkansas is the oldest national park maintained by the US National Park Service and, as the name suggests, is known for its natural hot springs. The springs are open to the public for bathing, and the park has a collection of bathhouses dating from various ages of American history.

Believed to have natural medicinal and healing abilities, seeking out and enjoying natural hot springs is an everyday activity. But this can be difficult; what if there was a way you could get some of the healing benefits of natural hot springs at home?

Swedish immigrants popularized Saunas in America, but this practice is similar to that of sweat lodges used in spiritual ceremonies of First Nations and Indigenous communities.

Whether you're interested in health benefits, meditation, or if you're looking to incorporate some 'me-time' into your new retirement routine, getting a good healthy sweat with some natural (or artificial) heat may be just the thing. There are many options: natural hot springs, saunas, sweat lodges, steam baths, or just heading to a spa for the day. After all, you've spent the last decades working hard, so why not find an interesting way to sink into a more relaxed lifestyle.

FLORIDA

In Florida, we will be taking on some group activities as hobbies. After all, you don't want to spend your golden years enjoying hobbies all by yourself.

DRIVE-IN THEATERS

Some parts of American culture have been left by the wayside, they fell behind as time marched on.

The classic drive-thru restaurant, video rental stores, roller rinks, and big screen drive-in movies are a few examples. You can still find them here and there, but most seem to have disappeared from the landscape. Finding and visiting these icons of the American past can make an interesting hobby, giving you a reason to travel to places you would never have otherwise.

The Fort Lauderdale Swap Shop is one example of such a place-out-of-time that would make an excellent travel destination. With 14 screens, it is the world's largest drive-in theater and shows a mixture of modern and classic movies. While there, check out the arcade, flea market, and car museum to round out your sightseeing.

A little bit of inspiration can take even the most routine hobby, like catching a movie, into something you can become passionate about and use as an excuse to see more of America.

GROUP FITNESS

You might think retirement is the time to start winding down, take it easy, and avoid straining yourself too much.

Alternatively, you may know that maintaining your strength and physical fitness is the key to staying healthy and independent. But if you're bored of the same old gym routine or relaxing walks around the neighborhood aren't keeping you in shape, group fitness classes might be a thing to explore.

Meeting new people, getting motivated, and pushing yourself harder will keep those endorphins flowing. One example of a group fitness class suitable for any age or fitness level is OrangeTheory Fitness. Established in Fort Lauderdale in 2010, the intensity of the workout is based on your own heart rate and exertion level, so everyone can participate and see benefits. Many companies are promoting and experimenting with new group classes, and since hitting the gym may be part of your routine anyway, why not also meet some new people and see if a group class suits you!

GEORGIA

We'll look to the skies of the Peach State for our next few hobbies.

BUTTERFLY BREEDING

Callaway Resort & Gardens in Georgia is home to the Cecil B. Butterfly Center, where you can see over 1,000 species of these beautiful insects. But with a little effort, you can raise your butterflies at home. All you need is:

- a host plant where butterflies will lay eggs
- a small aquarium (a glass jar will also work)
- plants to create a caterpillar habitat

For most species, it takes less than a month to raise a butterfly from the egg stage through the caterpillar stage before it finally becomes a butterfly. While you'll have to release them back into the wild afterward, it is always an interesting journey, and seeing a caterpillar transform into a completely new form is always mesmerizing.

When done correctly, raising butterflies can help build up the local insect communities and doesn't harm the natural environment around you. Depending on where you live, there will be different native butterfly species, and some might require a helping hand. Here is a quick list of species that are easy to raise and the region of the US where they can be found[1].

- Anise Swallowtail (*Papilio zelicaon*) (Western U.S.)
- Giant Swallowtail (*Papilio cresphontes*) (Across U.S.)
- Eastern Black Swallowtail (*Papilio polyxenes asterius*) (Eastern U.S.; Arizona)
- Sleepy Orange (*Eurema nicippe*) (Southern U.S.)
- Checkered White (*Pontia protodice*) (North America)
- Becker's White (*Pontia beckeri*) (Western U.S.)
- Cabbage White (*Pieris rapae*) (North America)
- The Monarch (*Danaus plexippus*) (North America)
- The Queen (*Danaus gilippus thersippus*) (Western U.S.)
- Red Spotted Purple (*Limenitis astyanax astyanax*) (Midwest and Eastern U.S.)
- Lorquin's Admiral (*Limenitis lorquini burrisoni*) (Western U.S.)
- California Tortoiseshell (*Nymphalis californica*) (Western North America)
- Milbert's Tortoiseshell (*Nymphalis milberti furcillata*) (Western and N.E. U.S.)
- Satyr Comma (*Polygonia satyrus satyrus*) (Western United States)
- Red Admiral (*Vanessa atalanta rubria*) (North America)
- Painted Lady (*Vanessa cardui*) (North America)
- The Buckeye (*Junonia coenia grisea*) (Southern U.S.)
- Bordered Patch (*Chlosyne lacinia crocale*) (Southwestern U.S.)
- Gray Hairstreak (*Strymon melinus*) (North America)

Look up some pictures, see which ones might live in your climate and region, and ensure you have a camera ready.

A colourful blue and white butterfly[2]

PLANE SPOTTING

It might be a surprise to learn that Hartsfield-Jackson Atlanta International Airport in Georgia is the busiest airport in America, with over 350,000 flights every year[3]. That would be a great location to try your luck at plane spotting.

Like bird watching, plane spotters try to identify and track specific planes visually. Most try to see as many different types of planes as possible, and many also have a favorite type (like private jets or a specific brand of a commercial airliner) they set out to look for.

The hobby will start rather easily as you check off common planes that show up at your local airport. But as you progress, you'll end up learning about different types of planes, where they show up and why, and you will have to start getting creative to give yourself a chance to spot a new or rare aircraft.

Details on aircraft appearance, registrations, and general flight plans can be found online so you can stalk your favorite aircraft. Prime locations for plane spotting like airports, air shows, or aviation museums can make great travel destinations too.

Of course, if planes aren't your favorite type of vehicle, you can try similar hobbies like trainspotting, bus spotting, or even satellite spotting.

One last word of caution, trying to plane spot near military facilities or in foreign countries can potentially get you into some trouble with the authorities, so make sure to check in advance that showing up with binoculars and a notepad won't get you mistaken for a spy!

KENTUCKY

You can get the word out with these hobbies from Kentucky.

SONG WRITING

We might not all be rockstars, but it's probably safe to say that everybody has at least one good song inside them. Maybe it's a tune you always seem to hum to yourself, a few favorite phrases or rhymes, or even some unique memories that tell a great story.

It doesn't have to be complicated; after all, what is the most well-recognized song in the English language? Why 'Happy Birthday,' of course.

Written by a pair of native Kentuckian sisters, Patty and Mildred Hill, in 1893, this simple song is known worldwide and is probably the one that everybody regularly sings.

So what are the basic parts of writing a song? Remember, you don't have to master all these parts; many songwriters focus on their specific strengths and collaborate with others to create the finished product.

. . .

Introduction

This is usually just instrumentals, with no lyrics, and is the build up to the song. Make sure to get your audience excited to hear what comes next.

Verse

This is where the details of your song live. If you're telling a story or presenting a message, you'll probably want to express it in the lyrics of each verse.

Chorus

Also called a refrain, this is the part of a song that repeats itself. It usually shows up between verses, and a catchy chorus makes your song easy to sing along with.

Melody

This is the basic 'tune' of your song. It can vary between verses and between the verses and chorus.

Harmony

This is how the instruments combine and mix to create the overall sound. Different supporting sounds in the harmony can drastically change the feel of the melody, even if it is repeated in the same way.

Rhythm

If you were to clap along to your song, you would clap on the beats of the rhythm. This can refer to the speed (usually called tempo) as well.

These aren't the only elements of a song, and the study of music is a much larger topic than you might think. Once you get your feet wet with some basics, you can start learning the theory behind crafting songs of a particular style or how to achieve specific emotions or feelings with sounds. This can be a very rewarding hobby.

SOCIAL MEDIA

If you started a conversation saying that your new retirement hobby was 'social media,' you might see many disapproving faces.

Social media is often seen as a waste of time, a bad habit, or worse. And while those people may have a point, there is no reason you can't find a positive online community that enriches your life or, even better, start your own. No social media platform is inherently good or bad; it's what we make of it.

A survey of social media users from 2020 found that Kentuckians were the most connected online[1]. So what makes a good online community that adds to your life instead of draining from it?[2]

- Show gratitude - if people offer their advice, remember that they took the time to respond and contribute.
- Give praise - when members take on roles (like a moderator), those can be difficult and time-consuming, but online communities don't work well without these volunteers.
- Stay positive - while everyone likes to vent and complain, communities built on these negative principles don't usually positively impact their members' lives.
- Build relationships - a comforting thing about being online is being anonymous; however, that removes people from the real-world consequences of their thoughts and actions. Treat the people on the other side of your screen like actual people.
- Encourage creativity - most members of online communities don't actively participate; they just read everyone else's comments and input. Encourage everyone to join in and contribute, or the community will stagnate.
- Relax - sticking to strict rules and having serious arguments can slowly snowball into toxic problems. Keep things lighthearted, and a little humor goes a long way.

- Don't get angry - think before responding to comments that frustrate you. Many online people, called trolls, will deliberately start arguments and pick fights online. Avoid getting roped in, and don't take the bait if someone is looking for a fight.

LOUISIANA

Since America is a melting pot of different cultures, in Louisiana, we'll pull influences from around the world and improvise them into something new.

JAZZ APPRECIATION

New Orleans is the birthplace of jazz, a truly American art form. The key element that sets jazz apart from other styles of music is improvisation. Once you've learned the traditional rules of music, you can begin to appreciate how a great jazz musician can bend, break, and play with those rules to capture and surprise the audience.

While jazz music isn't everyone's cup of tea, just like tea, you might have to find your favorite flavor before you can really enjoy it. Here is a quick primer on the different styles of jazz music. Give a few different ones a try; you might just be surprised!

- Swing jazz, or big band jazz - involves a large group of musicians, and the improvisation comes in the form of regular

individual solos throughout the song. This music tends to be easy to dance to and is very approachable.
- Bebop - this is where jazz became more challenging, with more of a focus on individual artists with distinct styles. More complicated rhythms, melodies, and chord progressions mean it might take some time to get familiar with Bebop jazz, and you might only really enjoy the performances of specific musicians.
- Afro-Cuban - With influences from Latin and Cuban culture, this style has some very distinctive rhythms that get your body moving.
- Dixieland - The classic New Orleans style usually includes trumpets, trombones, clarinets, and a two-beat rhythm. More focused on the ensemble as a whole than individual soloists, this is often thought of as traditional jazz music.
- Jazz-funk - Electrified sounds and a grooving beat with a hint of Jamaican reggae. There is less improvisation, but a wide array of influences from R&B, soul, and even disco can be found here.

FUSION CUISINE

Louisiana is home to African, Creole, Acadian, and Isleño cultures, not to mention a half-dozen or more Indigenous groups. They co-exist and have created a unique environment in Louisiana, something that is more than the sum of its parts. If they look back far enough, many Americans will find a diverse blend of cultures and histories in their family tree. Putting the pieces of these cultures together in a way that respectfully celebrates them all would be a great hobby. So how would you go about doing this? First, you would need to research your family's past. While genealogy is a hobby, how will you combine these cultures?

Fusion cuisine combines flavors and techniques from multiple cultures. After becoming popular in the 1970s, fusion restaurants and dishes can now be found across the USA. It can be tricky to combine flavors from different regions of the world on your own, but using cooking techniques from one area with the flavors of another can have surprising (and tasty) results.

To invent an exciting new fusion recipe, you don't have to be a five-star chef. Here are some starting tips to help you dream up a masterful creation:

- What cooking techniques do you know or want to learn?
- What types of restaurants or regional cuisines do you enjoy?
- What are your favorite herbs and spices you like to add to your food?

Combine your answers to those questions differently and record which of your experiments worked the best. Here are two fusion recipe examples to get you started.

Philly Bulkogi Eggroll[1]

Ingredients

- 2 lb beef (Bulgogi), thinly sliced
- ½ onion, sliced
- 12 egg roll wrappers
- 12 slices of American cheese
- 1 egg, beaten
- oil for deep frying

Bulgogi Mix

- 5 tbsp soy sauce
- 4 tbsp brown sugar
- 4 tbsp asian pear
- 2 tsp Korean toasted sesame oil
- 2 stalks green onion, minced

- 6 tsp garlic, chopped
- 2 tbsp roasted sesame seeds
- ¼ tsp dried red pepper flakes
- salt and pepper to taste
- garnish: sesame seeds

Directions

- Marinate thinly sliced ribeye steak with Korean bbq marinade with onions. (Min 4 hrs)
- Cook bulgogi meat and cool and set to the side.
- Get 8 egg rolls wrappers and put 1 slice of American cheese and 2 ounces of cooled bulgogi and wrap firmly.
- Fry egg rolls at 350 for 3-5 minutes until golden brown.
- Cut in half and serve!

Mexican Lasagna[2]

Ingredients

- 1 pound lean ground beef
- 2 jars (15 to 16 ounces each) medium salsa
- 1 can (15 ounces) black beans, drained and rinsed
- 1 can (8 3/4 ounces) whole kernel corn, drained
- 4 teaspoons chili powder
- 3 teaspoons Oregano Leaves, divided
- 2 teaspoons ground cumin
- 2 eggs
- 2 containers (15 ounces each) ricotta cheese
- 2 cups (8 ounces) shredded Mexican blend cheese, divided
- 9 lasagna noodles, uncooked

Directions

- Preheat oven to 350°F. Brown ground beef in a large skillet on medium-high heat. Drain fat. Add salsa, beans, corn, chili powder, 2 teaspoons of the oregano, and cumin; mix well.
- Bring to a boil. Reduce heat to low; simmer for 5 minutes.
- Beat eggs in a large bowl. Add ricotta cheese, 1 cup of the Mexican blend cheese, and remaining 1 teaspoon oregano; mix well.
- Spread about 1 cup of the meat sauce onto the bottom of a 13x9-inch baking dish; top with 3 noodles. Spread 1/2 of the cheese mixture over the noodles. Repeat the meat sauce, noodles, and cheese layer once. Top with remaining noodles and meat sauce, making sure to cover noodles with sauce. Sprinkle with remaining 1 cup Mexican blend cheese. Cover with foil.
- Bake for 45 minutes, then remove foil. Bake 15 minutes longer or until noodles are tender. Let stand 15 minutes before serving.

MISSISSIPPI

The Mississippi River is the most significant influence behind the two hobbies here, with activities from the original Aboriginal Mississippians and early American pioneers.

RIVERBOAT CRUISING

It used to be quite the stereotype that once you hit a certain age, the only travel you would be able to manage was an ocean cruise or an all-inclusive resort. While it's true that most people of retirement age aren't backpacking around Europe and sleeping in hostels, there is definitely a middle ground.

Instead of that cruise or all-inclusive, where you don't always get to experience much except the resort itself, why not try a riverboat cruise? Mississippi riverboats have a long and storied past, with steamships traveling up and down the river since 1811.

Stopping off to see the local sights, joining in on some high-stakes card games, and having a relaxing pace set by the river are just a few things to enjoy. These river cruises can range from ultra-luxury boats like a five-star hotel down to the equivalent of a tour bus focused on getting you to your next destination on time. So whether you are more of a 'journey' or a 'destination' person, why not avoid the airports, hotels, and busy beaches and give a river cruise a try.

POTTERY

Before the European settlers arrived, the Indigenous peoples of America had rich and varied cultures. The original Mississippians, known to live around the eponymous river since at least as far back as the 800s, had a lifestyle based almost entirely on what could be obtained from the river and its banks.

Mississippian pottery had a unique style. They used shells from the river to temper their pottery, which prevented shrinkage and cracking while the pottery dried. While not as smooth or elaborate as other cultures of the time, the ground-up mussel shells incorporated into the material gave Mississippian pottery a unique look and texture.

The way ancient peoples used the resources around them tells us a lot about their daily life and how they lived. We can learn what was important to them and gain insight into how they saw the world.

So if you decide to start dabbling in pottery, a fairly common hobby, maybe you could take things a step further and use it to tell a story about how you live your life. What ingredients could you incorporate from the world around you into your starting materials or designs? Is there a deeper story to tell with the pottery's shape or color? Is there a spiritual or meaningful purpose behind how you will use this pottery?

The difference between taking a pottery class or two and churning out a few cups and ashtrays before moving on to the next thing, and putting some thought and meaning into your designs is the difference between an everyday activity and a genuine hobby. Even though everybody has to start with the basics, going into pottery knowing you have an end goal in mind, to create a piece of art where every element is meaningful to you and represents something you care about, is a much more fulfilling way to think about this, and all of the other hobbies in this book.

SOUTH CAROLINA

Our hobbies from South Carolina are all about getting inspiration from the earth.

SAND ART

Many of us will have fond memories of building sand castles at the beach as young children. While they only lasted until the next big wave knocked them over or the tide came in, making art with only sand and water can get fairly complicated. Even though it's seen as a children's activity, there are enough skills for you to master that it's possible to dive into this hobby. And if the temporary nature of sand art bothers you, modern technology means you can always document your favorite works of art with photos and video.

Sand castles are the most well-known form of sand art, and America's largest sand castle was built on Myrtle Beach in South Carolina in 2007. It was almost 50 feet tall and was created over ten days using 300 truckloads of sand. In theory, sand castles are pretty simple; add the right amount of water to the sand so that it sticks together. You can use combinations of buckets, shovels, and whatever creative implements you can think of to create details. Some sand castle enthusiasts also use metal straws, woodworking tools, melon ballers, spatulas, or paint brushes to make truly spectacular creations.

An elaborate sand castle

If building upwards isn't appealing, you can also create flatter designs in the sand. Sand raking is the art of using a rake to create patterns and designs in the sand. You may have seen something similar in a zen garden, and basic bamboo rakes are great for creating sand art. Sand raking is similar to creating crop circles (but without annoying any farmers), and if you know of any empty beaches, you can find yourself a large canvas to work with. Geometric patterns, murals, and many other designs can be created by contrasting the dry, light-colored sand at the undisturbed surface and the wet, darker-colored sand below.

CARNIVOROUS PLANTS

Many master gardeners believe that speaking to their plants, giving them names, and playing soothing music help them grow. Their years of experience and green thumbs allow them to see some personality in plants by comparing the differences in how they grow and blossom, but for the rest of us, plants might mostly all seem the same.

Carnivorous plants, on the other hand, appear to have instant personality. While mercilessly chomping down on prey might not be the friendliest or approachable of personality traits, it's at least something to work with. That venus flytrap crunching on a slug could be a helpful friend trying to keep your home and garden pest free, or that pitcher plant could be a devious architect trapping bugs in a one-way biological maze for their own amusement. Give them a creative name, do your part by supplying the correct soil and regular watering, and you might find it a bit easier to relate to these houseplants compared to your traditional herbs and flowers.

Here are some common indoor carnivorous plants you can keep as a low-maintenance pet:

- Venus Flytrap - one of the most common carnivorous plants, eats flies, ants, slugs, and tiny insects. It likes damp soil and only needs to be fed a few times a month. The distinctive shape and mechanical snap of the trap make this a satisfying plant to grow.
- Pitcher Plants - these beautiful plants have a small pool of digestive juice within their pitcher structure formed by their leaves. They can have beautiful yellow and purple coloring and may be the most attractive of the carnivorous plants as they try to lure insects to their doom. The Cobra Lily is an incredibly striking example and looks like a snake ready to pounce.

- Butterwort - you might not even recognize these as carnivorous, at least not until you see the small flies trapped on its sticky leaves. It grows well in poor soil (don't add any fertilizer) but does need hotter temperatures, usually around 75°F.

TENNESSEE

Tennessee has a rich history that is reflected in these next two hobbies.

COUNTRY MUSIC

A genuinely American art form, the capital city of country music is Nashville, Tennessee. With humble roots at the start of the 20th century, it has changed and evolved along with our country during this time.

Jimmie Rodgers was the 'father of country music' with his guitar and distinctive vocals. The rise of Western Swing added drums, steel guitar, and some influence from jazz and big band music. Then Lester Flatt came along and sparked the height of the mountain bluegrass style. As it became popular, Roy Rogers and the influence of Hollywood cowboy movies began making country music mainstream.

Separate subgenres like Hank Williams' honky tonk and the more modern storytelling style songs from early Nashville started showing up. Fearing becoming too 'soft,' outlaw country tried to return country music to its roots with the likes of Willie Nelson. This didn't last long, and in the late 1980s, superstars like Garth Brooks and Alan Jackson returned country to the popular music scene. And today, modern country music has been heavily influenced by pop music trends.

Whew, that was a lot. So what are the basic elements that make country music 'country music?'

- Based on the folk style of the southern US or western style, cowboys
- Has a strong narrative in the lyrics
- Accompanied by string instruments like guitars, fiddles, or banjos
- Uses simple chord progressions that are easy to follow along with

VOLUNTEERING

Tennessee is known as the volunteer state. While that name comes from their military history and supplying militia soldiers, that's not the type of volunteering we recommend as a retirement hobby.

Many people feel a loss of purpose in their life after ending their career, as they become unsure of their role in society and don't have a schedule or direction. Volunteering can give people that sense of purpose back, and the best way to give yourself a reason to get up in the morning is to have a good cause that relies on you.

Most of us have volunteering on our list of things we'll do when we have more time, but not everyone manages to follow through. Why is that? If you are one of those people that have been 'meaning to get around to thinking about choosing a place to start maybe volunteering soon...' here are some slightly selfish reasons to get started today.

Volunteering benefits you by[1,2]:

- Improving your mental health,

- Increasing life satisfaction,
- Boosting social well-being,
- Reducing your risk of high blood pressure,
- Cutting down stress, and
- Gives you a chance to be physically active

So next time you need some motivation to get off the couch and help other people or support a good cause, remember that you're also helping yourself!

WEST VIRGINIA

Let's head to West Virginia, where we can take some trips to different places and times.

TRAVELING THE 'WORLD'

What if you could travel to the most famous cities in the world without a passport or a plane ticket? There are many reasons why you might not be able to spend your retirement traveling the globe and joining the jet set.

And while taking virtual tours from the comfort of your own home could also be a great hobby, sometimes you need an excuse to hit the road and head somewhere famous, or at least somewhere famous sounding...

For example, if you could manage a road trip to West Virginia, you could stop by Athens, Cairo, Glasgow, Shanghai, and Vienna while you're there.

America is full of places named after other, more exotic locales; here's a quick list to get you started:

- Melbourne is in Australia, and Kentucky
- Luxembourg is in Belgium and Wisconsin
- Halifax is in Canada and Missouri
- Havana is in Cuba and Illinois
- Copenhagen is in Denmark and New York
- Paris is in France and Texas
- Dublin is in Ireland and New Hampshire
- Lima is in Peru and Ohio
- Seville is in Spain and Florida

BLACKSMITHING

Coal mining is the soul of West Virginia, with deposits spread almost everywhere across the mountainous state. It has been one of the primary industries in the region, bringing prosperity to the state for over a century. So how could West Virginians incorporate coal into their hobbies?

The ideal fuel for a blacksmith's forge is bituminous coal. Reaching temperatures of 3,500°F, the forge heats metals until they can be shaped and worked into their final forms. This is the same type of coal found in West Virginia, making it an ideal hobby.

Some easy-to-learn beginner blacksmithing projects could be bracelets, coat hooks, kitchen utensils, or letter openers. Basic shapes won't require too much skill but can still be impressive and practical.

Here is a quick list of equipment you would need to get started:

- An anvil and a forge,
- Hammers with flat and curved striking faces,
- Tongs for holding hot materials,
- Chisels and punches for cutting metal and creating holes, and most importantly,
- A safe place to smith and any recommended safety equipment

Unlike many other hobbies in this book, you will probably need professional instruction to learn the basics, and it might take longer to master the necessary skills.

Unfortunately, that means there is a more significant upfront financial and time investment to start learning to become a blacksmith. On the other hand, amateur blacksmithing has become more prevalent in recent years, so there is a growing body of resources, books, videos, and guides available for new beginners to carry on this traditional craft.

MIDWEST

ILLINOIS

Whether you want to build a replica of the past or catch a glimpse of the future, the hobbies of Illinois have got you covered.

MODEL TRAINS

For over 40 years, the town of Wheaton, Illinois, has hosted the Great Midwest Train Show. Every year, people come to display their trains, show off new models, take workshops to learn the ins and outs of model railroads, and buy whatever bits and pieces they are missing to create their miniature worlds.

While there is an appeal in creating a model town with its own working railroad, it can be a daunting hobby to get started in. Where do you get the trains, do you build the town yourself, what about all the electrical connections and controls? But whenever a hobby seems too complicated, think of it as an opportunity. There will always be more to learn and ways to improve your work, so you'll never get bored! To get you started, here are some key questions to think about:

- What scale will you build at? The scale is written as a ratio of the model's proportions compared to the original. A common scale in the United States is 1:160 (also called the N scale), which gives train cars between 3 and 4 inches long. You can select your scale based on your space and the available models in your area.
- Don't forget to ensure all the cars on each train have the same connectors or couplers so they can attach.
- What type of track will you use? The space between the two tracks is called the gauge. It is better to pick one size gauge for all your trains in the scene. There are also different standards for model railway parts to ensure everything fits together properly.
- What landscape do you want? Model railroads don't just sit on a table; most hobbyists also build a scene around the trains, either a real location or something from their imagination. You can purchase model pieces or kits (such as buildings, trees, people, and decorations) or try to create these yourself from balsa wood, plastic, or cardboard.
- What will make the trains move? While a static model is easier, it would be a waste to put all that effort into creating a beautifully detailed landscape full of your favorite trains and never see them move. Most beginners should start with electric models, which can run power through the rails or use batteries in the trains. More advanced hobbyists might try their hand at steam or combustion engine models, but these can get complicated, large, and rather expensive for a beginner.

And remember, just like most other hobbies, sometimes just a little tweaking is all it takes to turn something from a hobby that only seems mildly interesting into a full-blown passion. If trains aren't your favorite, consider ships, cars, historical battles, or whatever models you can find at your local hobby shop.

TAROT CARD READING

Tarot cards have been around since the 1400s in Europe, but we can trace the more familiar modern American version back to Eden Gray. She was a Chicago-born actress who turned the occult craft of tarot card reading into the contemporary version we see today associated with the 1960s counterculture. Her books on the subject are likely responsible for much of the current interest in tarot reading and are the basis for how many practitioners interpret their cards. Her final book, '*Mastering the Tarot: Basic Lessons in an Ancient, Mystic Art*' would be a fascinating place to start learning about tarot.

Tarot readers, also called cartomancers, interpret the 78 cards of their deck to divine the future, seek guidance from beyond, or help with their spiritual growth. The cards each have one of 22 symbols, or arcana, associated with it, and there are a half-a-dozen or so common variations of the tarot deck.

While dabbling in the occult may not be everyone's cup of tea, tarot readings can be a friendly, social activity more often associated with psychics and magicians rather than satanic beliefs. A typical tarot reading might sound more like a friendly conversation than a serious prophecy. The reader and listener use the cards drawn to guide their discussion and pull out truths that would remain otherwise hidden. If you enjoy striking up conversations with strangers, this could be the perfect hobby to make use of those talents. Similar arts, like reading someone's palm or tea leaves in a cup, use almost the same skills, so I'm sure you can find something that fits your personality.

You could perform readings for friends or strangers, in person or online, or add your flair and expression. First, do some background research, find a tarot reader to help you learn the ropes, practice with some close friends, and then most importantly, come up with a mystical stage name. Anyone might have the gift for divination, so it couldn't hurt to find out.

INDIANA

Everything in life requires balance, a ying for every yang, so to speak. So in Indiana, the hobbies will start fast and furious, and then we'll switch it up and balance that out by taking it nice and slow.

AMATEUR RACING

If you were to ask a room full of people what the most famous car race is, I bet you more than a few would say the Indianapolis 500. Even if you've never been interested in the sport, you probably know the name and can easily imagine the sights and sounds of race day. The roaring engines, black smoke, the smell of fuel, and the cheering crowd as they race across the finish line. While it would be more than a mild understatement to say that retirement is not the ideal time to start a career as a race-car driver, amateur racing could be just the hobby for you.

When most people think of amateur car racing, they imagine famous actors, European soccer stars, or wealthy business owners pulling up to a modern race track in a brand new bright red sports car that costs more than the average person's house. But amateur racing isn't just a hobby for ultra-rich playboys with a death wish; it can be a fun, affordable, and most importantly, safe activity.

To keep this hobby at a modest budget accessible to most regular folk, let's look at the best options if you have a (relatively reasonable) need for speed.

Karting: While you might have visions of children's birthday parties or amusement parks, a wide range of go-karts can meet anyone's skill level or speed. Whether you own the kart yourself or just rent one to do a few laps at the local course on the weekend, this is an affordable option that lets you experience the thrill of racing without worrying about damaging an expensive vehicle of your own.

Autocross: Imagine an empty parking lot, or maybe an abandoned airfield, with a racecourse marked with traffic cones. There are no walls to crash into, no competitors grinding against your tires or even any requirements for special licenses or training. You can show up, pay an entrance fee, and take whatever car you have around the track. This is a solo event; the goal is to see who can get the best time. Competitors are divided into different classes based on the type of cars and the number of race modifications made. Still, there isn't any reason you can't use your everyday vehicle. Remember that your times will be better if you first empty the groceries out of the trunk. A bit of friendly competition and a low bar to entry makes this a great way to see if auto racing is up your alley.

24 Hours of LeMons: If you are looking for something a little more elaborate but much less serious, the 24 hours of Lemons (named after the slightly more prestigious 24 Hours of Le Mans race) is a series of endurance races held regularly across the USA. Entry is restricted to cars worth less than $500, excluding any additional safety gear, and their slogan encapsulates the whole experience: "Racing's not just for rich idiots. Racing's for all idiots. (This includes you)." Register, sign onto a team, and you're on your way to a memorable experience.

TECHNOLOGY FREE

While some of us have trouble keeping up-to-date with technology, others have trouble disconnecting from devices. Suppose you find yourself in the second group. Why not look to the Amish, a society with a large population in Indiana that has chosen not to adopt many modern technological conveniences. This isn't just out of stubbornness or religious beliefs; the Amish value family time, face-to-face interaction, and self-sufficiency.

So how can we make this into a hobby? Maybe you could pick a few activities you already do where you rely on modern technology but where an old-fashioned or traditional option is available. Or you could make a habit of 'technological downgrading' on certain days of the week. Maybe it starts as a challenge, but you might start to notice the more relaxed pace and deliberateness of your actions is good for your soul. Slowing down and appreciating life is never a waste of time! Trying out old ways of doing things, whether it's housework, cooking, repairing, or communicating, can open your eyes. You may find you enjoy your new Amish ways more than relying on modern conveniences.

Here are a few examples of technological trade-ins to give you some ideas:

- Writing letters instead of emails
- Walking or biking instead of driving
- Reading physical books instead of ebooks or being on social media
- Shopping at local stores instead of online
- Physical puzzles or board games instead of phone games
- Cooking over a fire instead of using a stove or an oven

IOWA

Making old things new again is what's happening on our trip through Iowa. Whether it's adding a new modern twist on an old favorite or taking a second look at the amazing structures around us, we might have taken for granted.

ELECTRIC BIKES

The Great American Rail-Trail is a combined hiking and biking trail that passes through 12 states (including Iowa)[1]. It is a work in progress and is currently being built, with most trails located on old railway right-of-ways. About 50% longer than the Tour de France once completed; that will be one long bike ride! Luckily, new advances in battery and motor technology have made electric bikes much more accessible to the general public so that you can get a little help on your journey.

Peddle on your own for as long as you like; if you get a little bit tired (or need some help with those hills,) turn on the juice and make life a little easier and more enjoyable. Long-distance cycling is a well-established hobby, and almost anywhere you look in America, you'll find remarkably maintained trails and roads suitable for bicycles. However, biking does take a certain degree of fitness, and it can be intimidating if you haven't been on two wheels since grade school. While I'm sure you remember how (it's like riding a bike, after all,) the idea of getting all geared up for a ride and then collapsing from exhaustion after 10 minutes does make the whole ordeal a little less appealing.

Most e-bikes have ranges between 20 and 100 miles, depending on the model and how much pedaling you're doing. That means that even if you're getting your legs back in shape, you can still get around and see the sites for a fair distance.

A quick word of caution, though, e-bikes can be heavy. While the technology is improving every year, they still weigh 40 pounds or more, so they can be tricky to move around and difficult to manage if you fall or are less stable. Never fear, though; if that is a concern, there are always three-wheeled models.

So now that you are out of excuses, get yourself a new bike, get back on the pavement, and remember what it felt like to have the wind blowing in your face as a child, with your legs (and a charged battery) taking you wherever you wanted to go.

ARCHITECTURE APPRECIATION

It's hard not to reference famous books and movies when we think about or describe American culture. The classics of literature and the silver screen are the lenses through which most of us (and most of the world) see our country. Whenever I think of Iowa, for some reason, one of the first thoughts that jump to my mind is the book (and the movie) 'The Bridges of Madison County.' In this story, one of the main characters is a photographer traveling around Iowa, capturing images of the famous covered bridges.

While America might not have the oldest architecture in the world, it is home to so many local styles, and solutions to unique problems that understanding the principles behind these superb structures and visiting these impressive buildings could make for an interesting hobby. There are bold, amazing structures in almost every city that are not just interesting to appreciate, but it can be satisfying to learn about how they were built and why. There's no reason you couldn't take a hint from that famous book and try visiting and photographing them too.

After all, most of us have probably heard of the famous American architect Frank Lloyd Wright or maybe even had the chance to see one of his buildings in person. And almost anyone could appreciate the genius and style behind structures like the Golden Gate Bridge in San Francisco, the triangular Flatiron building in Chicago, the Empire State Building in New York, the Jefferson Memorial in Washington, or the Gateway Arch of St. Louis.

Sometimes the best hobbies involve taking a closer look and appreciating the things we see daily. Keeping your sense of wonder for all the amazing things humans can and will accomplish is a great way to keep your mind and spirit feeling young, well into your retirement years!

KANSAS

While it may not be the healthiest food on the planet, American cuisine might be the most comforting. Two food-related hobbies will showcase the state of Kansas; remember everything in moderation.

KANSAS STYLE BARBEQUE

Ok, this isn't much of a hobby on its own (sorry), but more of an example. All across America, there are local foods and also local food rivalries. Learning about the regional variations in popular foods, choosing your favorite version, and learning to perfect it would be an interesting way to make food into a hobby.

Some examples of food rivalries to explore...

Barbeque - Alabama (with white sauce), Kansas-city (with tomato and molasses sauce), Memphis (dry pork ribs), North Carolina (pulled pork with vinegar sauce), St Louis (grilled not smoked), or Texas (with beef instead of pork)

Pie - Boston cream (custard or creme filling coated in chocolate), Chess (sweet custard with lemon, orange, or chocolate flavoring), Derby (chocolate and walnut), Key lime (with meringue topping), Mississippi mud pie (chocolate), Pecan, Shaker lemon, Shoofly (molasses), Strawberry rhubarb, Sweet potato, and of course Apple (with or without a slice of cheese?)

Hot Dogs - Carolina (chili, slaw, and onions), Chicago (onions, relish, and mustard), Coney Island (chili, mustard, and onions), Seattle (cream cheese, onions, or sauerkraut), New York White Hot (unsmoked, so it has a white color)

Pizza - Chicago (deep crust with sauce on top of the cheese), Detroit (square), New York (thin and sold by the slice), Quad-City (spicy tomato sauce with toppings under the cheese and cut into strips), St. Louis (made with Provel cheese and a thin crust)

And a bunch of other options, like sandwiches, ice creams, salads, seafood, chili, soups... Take your time and find your favorites from across America!

POTLUCK

Potluck is a midwest tradition thought to be derived from the Indigenous 'potlatch' ceremony. It is a communal meal where everyone brings a homemade dish to share. People get a chance to show off their specialties or secret family recipes, and they have been bringing families and communities together since the dawn of American history.

But these events don't just happen. While churches and community groups might organize a monthly get-together, there is no reason you can't take some initiative and put together a regular event for your own community. To get you started with an authentic Kansas-style potluck recipe, here is how you can make a bacon cheeseburger tater-tot casserole[1]:

Ingredients

- 1 1/2 pounds ground beef
- ½ pound center-cut sliced bacon, cooked until crisp and crumbled
- 2 ½ cups shredded cheddar cheese
- 10-ounce can condensed cheddar cheese soup
- 16 ounces sour cream
- 32-ounce package of frozen tater tots, thawed (There will be some left over.)
- 2 scallions, chopped

Directions

- Preheat the oven to 350°F.
- In a large skillet over medium-high heat, cook beef until nicely browned and no pink remains; drain well.
- In a mixing bowl, combine cooked beef, crumbled bacon, cheddar cheese, soup, and sour cream; spread prepared mixture into a greased 8'x 8' baking dish. Top with tater tots, placing them in even rows over the filling, then gently spray tater tots with nonstick baking spray.
- Bake uncovered on the center rack for 40 to 45 minutes, or until the filling is hot and bubbly and the tater tots are golden brown.
- Garnish with shredded cheese, chopped bacon, and sliced scallions, if desired; serve at once.

MICHIGAN

Although Michigan is known for bordering the Great Lakes, we'll avoid the obvious and pick some more obscure hobbies from this great state.

LETTER WRITING

How would you feel if you got a long handwritten letter in the mail from a friend you hadn't seen in a while. Would you glance at it and throw it in the trash as you would with an email, or would you take some time, sit in a comfy chair and focus and enjoy reading it? Knowing the time and effort of writing a letter makes receiving one all the more special.

So why not spread that feeling to others and make a practice of handwriting some letters. Chances are there is a post office right around the corner from you, and even those of us living in the most remote locations have access to the US mail service. Even if you're working on a boat in the middle of the Detroit River in Michigan, you can receive mail under zip code 48222, which gets delivered to the only floating post office in the United States.

And after you get finished connecting with all of your far-away friends and family, you don't have to stop there. You could find a pen pal, write to people in other countries, or even send letters to your representatives in government and make your voice heard. Letters to the editor, thank you notes, and family updates mean there is never a shortage of people or topics to write about.

Get yourself a nice set of pens, fancy paper, and personalized envelopes, and turn your letter writing into an art form. Take your time and know that the person receiving this mail knows it's not really about what you wrote but the thought and time you put into reaching out to them.

COLLECTING VINYL

As they grow older and wiser, people notice that history repeats itself. People become enamored with old things and traditions long after they have gone out of style, with 'retro' fashions becoming popular again and again in regular cycles. Collecting old vinyl records has gone through a few cycles of popularity now, and while collecting old Motown R&B records from the heydays of Detroit is great for a hit of nostalgia, you might have other interests from your past.

Maybe it's 8-tracks, tapes, or even CDs? If music isn't your thing, you could look into something like VHS tapes. If literature is more your speed, then classic original print runs of your favorite books could be your thing. Whatever old media interests you, there is something magical about experiencing the music and movies of our childhood in the way we originally heard, saw, or read them.

Now back to those old records; if you decide to go down that route and already have a record player handy, what should you look for when scavenging for vinyl at flea markets, record stores, and garage sales?

- Judge by the cover - if the record sleeve is in great shape, that's a good early sign
- See the light - hold the record under a bright light and tilt it to look for scratches and damage
- Listen in - ask to hear the record before buying if possible
- Watch your speed - make sure the record's speed matches your record player

When you start collecting old objects, don't let your excitement get ahead. Instead, take your time, and cherish your purchases. A well-thought-out collection that you took a few years to build will always be more satisfying than blowing a lot of money on a weekend eBay binge.

MINNESOTA

After enduring the long cold winters, Minnesotans make sure to make the most of the summer months. Here are two outdoor hobbies that will get you out and enjoying the summer sunshine.

STANDUP PADDLE BOARDING

Standup paddle boarding started gaining in popularity around 2013 and has spread around America. Legend has it that a diehard Hawaiian surfer began to have trouble getting up and down on his board as he got older and began to use a canoe paddle to get himself out to the waves and glide around with less stress on his joints. The style caught on and has branched out, now becoming its own sport and not just a surfing style.

While it can be a bit of a workout, standup paddle boarding is a great way to improve your balance and core strength, which will benefit you in your later decades.

You also don't need to have a beachfront getaway to start paddle boarding. For example, Minnesota is home to over 14,000 lakes, and almost any still body of water is a great place to learn. As a bonus, paddle boards for lakes can be much smaller and easier to store than their ocean-going counterparts and take up much less room than a canoe, kayak, or small boat. Paddle boards are usually around ten feet long and can come in inflatable or portable versions.

So if you are looking for a water sport with a low physical barrier to entry, can be done on almost any body of water, and uses minimal equipment, standup paddle boarding may be your thing.

STATE FAIRS

The largest state fair in the USA is the Minnesota State Fair, which had an attendance of over 2.1 million people in 2019. So what can you do at a state fair? First, enjoy a stroll around, see the sights, and line up for some rides. But the main attraction is all of the competitions. Most state (and county) fairs have several competitions you could enter, judge, or volunteer to help organize. Even if you don't enter, being part of the event can feel energizing and is a great way to meet new interesting people.

Common competitions include baking, crafts, artwork, gardening, and agriculture. Still, many state fairs also have their signature competitions that could be unique hobbies of their own, like growing unusually shaped vegetables (Minnesota's Rice County), making ugly cakes (Iowa's Johnson County), grocery bagging (Iowa State), duct tape creations (Kansas State), and my favorite, the Banana Derby (Georgia State) where capuchin monkey jockey's race each other on dogs.

So head on down, and keep your eyes peeled for a new hobby, a twist on an existing hobby, or set your sights on getting that first-place blue ribbon.

108 | 101 WAYS TO ENJOY RETIREMENT ACROSS AMERICA

Entrant for the Banana Derby[1]

MISSOURI

It can get hot during the summer in America, and every state has its own special way of keeping cool and beating the heat. Missouri's are something special, though, and we'll look into these for the next two hobbies.

FOUNTAINS

Do you know what nobody ever really appreciates as they should? A good water feature. A well-done fountain, pond, or miniature waterfall feels so relaxing and tranquil that most people don't even notice that it's there. Instead, they feel like they belong and can add so much to a space. For example, there are over 200 fountains scattered around Kansas City, Missouri. From utilitarian watering holes for horses to restored Italian relics from the renaissance, each one tells a story and adds a bit of flair and charm to the surroundings.

So how can you go about creating and maintaining your very own water feature? Here are the steps to create a three-tiered water fountain using garden pots, rubber hoses, and a small pump.

1. Find three different size garden pots; lighter ones are easier to work with so long as they are strong enough that they don't deform when filled. The largest will be the base, getting smaller as you go up.
2. Drill a small hole on the side of the bottom (largest) pot big enough to fit the power plug for the pump through. After you've run the pump power cord through, create a watertight seal around it with silicone or epoxy putty.
3. Attach the pump to the inside of the bottom pot.
4. Drill holes in the center of the bottoms of the smaller two pots large enough to run your hose through.
5. Pick a spot for your fountain; it will be hard to move after the next step.
6. Once you've attached your pump (with a power cord reaching out of the bottom pot) and run your hose up through the middle pot and into the top pot, you can fill all three pots with nice-looking, flat stones.
7. Fill all of the pots with water, turn on the pump, and do some last-minute leveling so it all sits flat. Make sure it's not leaking too.
8. Kick back, relax, and enjoy the sounds of running water in your backyard.

TABLESCAPING

Sweet iced tea is a staple of southern hospitality. Served ice cold and flavored with fruit, this drink was actually introduced to America at the 1904 World's Fair in St. Louis, Missouri. Nothing is more refreshing when you've been walking outdoors in the heat and humidity. So how else can we adopt the southern hospitality symbolized by a cool sweet tea on a porch?

In recent years, tablescaping has started to become popular. We all know how much work can go into the presentation of a dinner table before guests arrive. Proper seating, floral arrangements, and centerpieces require a lot of work to make things comfortable and appealing for your guests. Tablescaping turns this into a bit of a competition. Entrants design a themed table for a dinner party for two or four guests.

What a great way to get ideas and practice your skills for being a host.

While tablescaping competitors may spend weeks designing their tables and getting all of the components organized, there's no reason you can't just get some inspiration from their efforts and pick up some nice touches. Of course, you can always go all in and join in on the competition yourself, becoming a master of dinner party preparations.

Whether you compete or take notes, tablescaping will give you ideas on how to best present your sweet tea or whatever drink you use to cool down when your guests arrive.

NEBRASKA

The hobbies of Nebraska are all about understanding and appreciating some of the common wildlife that lives all around us.

NON-VIOLENT HUNTING

The state animal of Nebraska is the deer, probably the most commonly hunted animal in America. Even if you're a bona fide vegan who would never hurt a fly and would never dream of killing an animal for sport, there is something to be said for the activity of going hunting. Something hard to express in words, an intangible part of the ritual that has been imprinted on our cultural DNA and must be experienced firsthand.

As hunters track and stalk these animals in their natural environment, they develop an understanding and connection with these creatures that the rest of us never feel. Woods that seem silent and unremarkable to us might be saying a lot, but you must immerse yourself in that environment before you can understand that language. Learning to read the signs of wildlife, listening for quiet movements between the trees, and breathing in that wild, earthy smell of nature makes the outdoors come alive.

So if most of the hunting experience happens before the trigger is pulled and an animal is sacrificed for food, why not stop there?

Heading out early in the morning, finding the best spot to watch and track your' prey,' getting close enough to take aim, and then lining up that perfect shot to get the satisfaction of a 'kill' without the violence.

Also called non-lethal hunting or green hunting, if you wanted to, you could use a camera to mimic the action of taking that shot and come home with a trophy, or you could capture the moment in your memory. Think of it as being in a similar spirit as catch-and-release fishing.

Even the commonplace deer you see in the local park will become a majestic creature you now fully understand and appreciate.

BEEKEEPING

Many people try their hand at gardening as their retirement hobby. While that is an excellent choice if you are looking for a quiet, relaxing hobby, it can be a bit physically demanding. If only you had a helper, or better yet, thousands of eager helpers that want nothing better than to see your flowers flourish!

First, you'll need to get yourself a beehive. If you're looking for a few assistants to do some pollination work, you can get by with a small bee shelter that gives bees a place to avoid the wind and rain. These can easily be tucked away on a balcony or sheltered corner. If you're going this route, you can spend some time learning how to place your bee house properly, then leave them alone to do their work.

On the other hand, if you plan to harvest some honey, you'll need something a little larger. Langstroth and top-bar hives are the most common honey bee hives and resemble a small box-shaped dresser that gives honeybees ample room to build their honeycombs. You'll probably also need some tools to work with the bees, extract their honey, and avoid getting stung too much.

If bees are common in your area, they might appear naturally in your hive, but you'll likely have to introduce them yourself. You may be able to order them online or contact another local beekeeper to see if they are willing to donate you a queen.

Remember to do some research and make sure whatever bees you are looking for can thrive in your area. Don't be shy about reaching out to local beekeeping organizations. You'll want some local advice about common species, common weather conditions, and other potential problems unique to your location. Remember, you are providing a home for living animals, so you'll need to take that responsibility seriously.

NORTH DAKOTA

We aren't all sipping margaritas at our beach villa on the coast of Spain during retirement; most of us will have to be a little more careful with our spending and budgeting. These hobbies from North Dakota will give you some ways to create something out of (almost) nothing.

PET ROCKS

There are many great reasons to have hobbies; they can keep your mind active, your body feeling young, and your spirit continuously refreshed. But not everything you do has to have some boring practical benefit to justify the time you spend on it. Sometimes all you need to get out of a hobby is a smile and maybe a good conversation starter. As many of us get older, we realize that not everything in life has to be taken so seriously, and we learn to appreciate the value of a good laugh.

Started as a joke by North Dakota native Gary Ross Dahl for people who wanted a low-maintenance pet, the pet rock was a fad for about six months in 1975 but has remained in our collective consciousness ever since. Official pet rocks were all shipped from the same beach in

Mexico in a box that doubled as a pet carrier (complete with air holes) and included a 30-page instruction manual with tips for care, feeding, and tricks you could teach your new pet.

While admittedly, there isn't much to this hobby beyond finding the perfect rock and giving it a suitable name, having a loyal pet rock can teach us all a lesson that will serve us well in retirement, one that was probably best stated by Oscar Wilde:

> "We should treat all the trivial things of life seriously and all the serious things of life with sincere and studied triviality."

Whatever you choose as your actual hobbies, it's never a bad idea to have something silly in your life that you take way too seriously.

IRIS FOLDING

This papercraft technique recreates the iris diaphragm of a camera lens, focusing attention on the center of a card, image, or decoration. What better hobby for the state at the center of the USA?

All you need are strips of colored paper, some tape, and something to cut with. But patience and a ruler might also come in handy.

Start by downloading a template for your iris-folding pattern. This will specify how much paper you need, in how many different colors, and will show you what the finished design will look like. Iris patterns come in various shapes, and you can make them larger or smaller as necessary to suit whatever finished product you have in mind.

In general, making these patterns follows these steps:

- Cutting out a design window, the iris pattern will fit inside this 'frame'
- Cutting out strips of colored or specialty paper
- Folding those strips in half

- Placing the template behind the design window (some painters or other removable tape can be helpful here)
- Laying the strips of colored paper, from outside to inside, alternating between each color
- Adding a cover over the middle hole and securing the strips with tape
- Flipping the project over and removing the template to see your finished work

There are many forms of papercraft, and if iris folding isn't your style, there will be something that catches your eye and can inspire you.

Card made with iris folding[1]

OHIO

The hobbies from the great state of Ohio may sound simple, but on their own would be enough for a lifetime of enjoyment.

LINE-DANCING

There can be a lot of pressure going out to dance. Finding a partner, coming up with impressive and creative moves, and maybe feeling self-conscious if you're out of practice.

Line-dancing solves most of those problems. Everyone in the group follows the same steps, which usually have easy-to-learn basics. This means that once you've got your handful of moves down, you can relax and focus on having a good time. In the 1960s, the Madison, a line dance originating in Columbus, Ohio, was very popular. Also famous from the movie *Hairspray*, here are the main steps for the dance:

1. Step left foot forward
2. Place right foot beside left foot (without any weight on it) and clap
3. Step back on right foot

4. Move left foot back and across the right foot
5. Move left foot to the left
6. Move left foot back and across the right

Watching a few videos and practicing in your living room is all you need to get started, and if the Madison isn't your favorite, there is a whole world of line dances to try out.

So if you are the type of person who likes to go out for a night of music but is too shy to get onto the dance floor, or just someone looking for some new moves, line-dancing might be the hobby for you.

SELF-HELP

Nobody is perfect, and we all have areas of our lives that could do with a bit of improvement. The people of Ohio are no exception, and the most popular self-help book for Ohioans in 2020 was 'Year of Yes' by Shonda Rhimes[1].

Self-help, or self-improvement, style books have slowly been gaining traction among American readers, although they have been around for decades. Whether you want to be more intelligent, more prosperous, or a more well-rounded person, there are probably a few dozen books to choose from to help you on your journey.

Trying to become a better person is the perfect unattainable goal for retirement. While you will never get that definite satisfaction of a job well done, you'll know that every day you are becoming a better version of yourself, and that is always a worthy pursuit. Whether your hobbies are looking outward into the world or, like this one looking inside, remember the Ohio state motto, which says, there is 'So Much to Discover'; you just have to keep looking!

SOUTH DAKOTA

PORTRAITURE

A portrait is an artistic representation of a person. While the first thing you might think of when somewhan says 'portrait' is a realistic oil painting, there aren't any strict definitions here. Classic examples are painting, photographs, and sculptures, but like most things in the art world, the only limit is your creativity. Cartoon caricatures, descriptive poems, abstract images, as long as you capture the subjects' likeness, personality, character, mood, or some combination of those elements, you're creating a portrait. And if you have enough self-confidence or can't find anyone to pose for your art project, you can try your hand at a self-portrait!

South Dakota is home to one of the most famous collections of portraits in America, Mount Rushmore. Four portrait sculptures of George Washington, Thomas Jefferson, Theodore Roosevelt, and Abraham Lincoln, each measuring 60 feet tall, were carved into the mountain between 1934 and 1939.

So what are the elements of making a successful portrait:

- The portrait should provide an emotional connection or reveal something about the subject
- Every element should be saying something about the person or providing some deeper meaning
- When in doubt, focus on their eyes; they are called the window to the soul for a reason
- Don't worry too much about trying to make a portrait look exactly like the person; this is a skill that takes artists years to develop, and if you have to cheat with some tracing to start with, that's ok; make sure to add some of your own artistic flourishes!

INDOOR WINTER SPORTS

Winters can be brutally cold in South Dakota and many other areas of the USA. While bears and some other wildlife can pass the winter hibernating in a comfy cave, it's not so easy for us humans. Spending a winter completely inactive and lounging around isn't the best option for your health. So what are the possibilities for some indoor winter activities? We'll call these 'sports,' but really, they're miniature versions of the real thing that don't require a lot of equipment or space (or ice rinks) and involve just enough movement to get your blood pumping during the winter months.

Air Hockey

The northern US states have co-opted hockey from their Canadian neighbors. Air hockey is a tabletop version played on an eight-foot table where a thin plastic puck floats on a layer of air from the table surface. Both players try to knock the puck into their opponents' goal using a striker, a mallet that sits on the table surface with a short handle. Games appear similar to the old video game Pong. As long as you watch your fingers (that puck is moving pretty fast), this game is an excellent test of dexterity and strategy.

Table Shuffleboard

This time the original game is from Scotland, as table shuffleboard is just a miniature version of curling. Players slide metal and weighted plastic pucks down a long wooden surface, and points are scored based on how close you can leave your pucks to the end of the board. Opposing players can knock their opponent's pucks off the board, leave pucks further from the end of the board as guards, or attempt bank shots between pucks. Adding a pinch of salt to the surface reduces the friction of the board, so the pucks slide just like they were on ice. This also makes them curve a bit, mimicking the way curling stones can bend around in the full-sized version of the game. Boards are usually around nine-feet long, and each player gets to throw four pucks each round.

WISCONSIN

The beauty of nature is unmatched, but there is no reason you can't tweak things a little to line up better with your own tastes. Whether it's shaping trees into works of art or refining milk into cheese, improving the bounties of nature is the focus of these Wisconsin hobbies.

TREE SHAPING

One benefit of getting older is learning to become more patient, and patience is a virtue in this next hobby, tree shaping. By shaping branches into unnatural forms over the years, grafting trees onto each other, or forcing branches and trunks to grow together in a process called inosculation (or self-grafting), artists can create beautiful shapes and forms out of trees.

Also called arborsculpture, this is an ancient hobby, starting with living root bridges in India, creating garden houses in the Middle East, or more common examples like creating hedge fences or walls.

Along with the shaping techniques, grafting and pruning are used to control the form of the tree. Two of the primary methods for shaping are instant shaping and gradual shaping.

Instant shaping is used with trees already 6 to 10 feet tall. The trees are bent or woven into the desired shape, then held in place with a cast or form. The actual shaping is instant, but the tree may have to be held in place for several years before the new shape is permanent.

Gradual shaping is used with young saplings less than a foot tall. The tree's growth is guided along a predetermined path, usually with a wooden jig or a wire frame. Adjustments might have to be made on a weekly basis and could take up to a decade before the tree reaches a mature stage, and the project is finished.

So what kind of artistic shapes can you grow?

One of the more interesting forms of tree shaping is creating living furniture, and the first known person to attempt this was John Krubsack. A Wisconsin farmer with a background in tree grafting, Grubsack designed and grew a chair from 32 maple boxelder saplings. The chair took 11 years to grow and was finally harvested in 1914 and is still displayed by his descendants to this day!

While growing your own chair might be a bit too complex for your first attempt at tree shaping, there is no limit to the creativity of potential tree shaping projects, which can be as simple as creating a nice-looking hedge over a few seasons, to growing an ambitious sculpture over a decade.

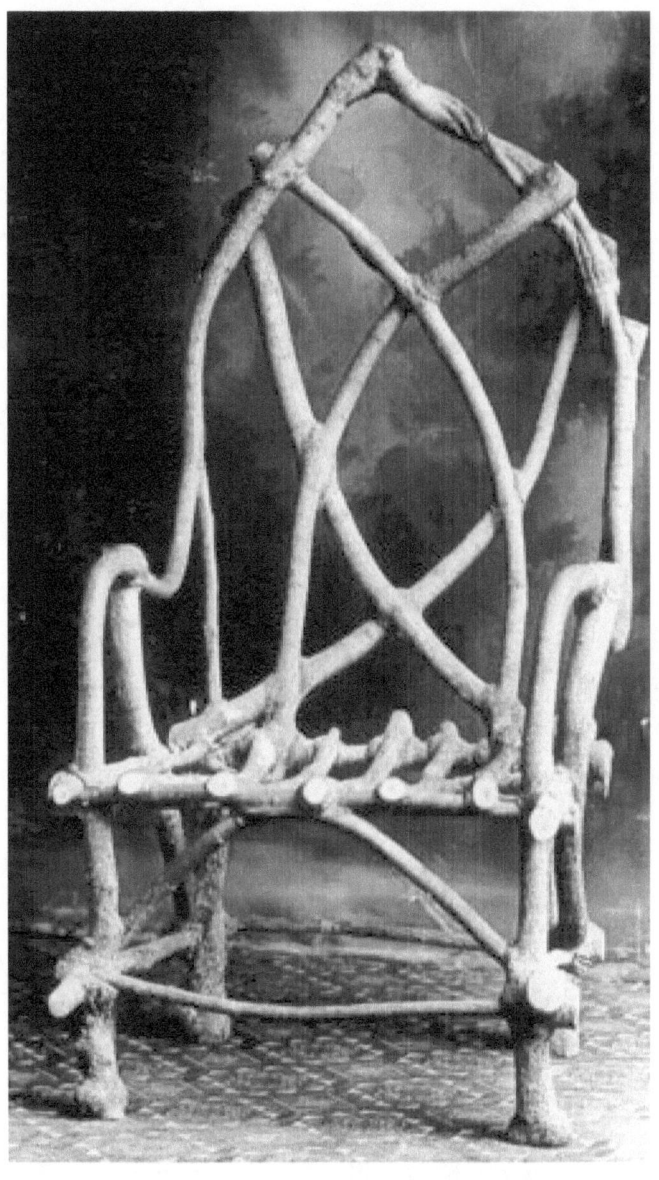

John Krubsack's chair

CHEESE MAKING

Known as America's Dairyland, Wisconsin is famous for the quantity and quality of the cheese it produces. Whether your favorite is a french-style Muenster, a creamy marbled-blue jack, or the Wisconsin staple Colby, there is a Wisconsin-made cheese for anyone (who isn't lactose intolerant).

While the award-winning cheeses of Wisconsin dairies might be hard to replicate at home, it can be surprisingly easy to create your own cheese. This can be as simple as an overnight recipe or complex and involve aging your homemade masterpiece for months.

Here are three examples of cheese you could try making with readily available ingredients in order of increasing difficulty.

Easiest - Farmer's Cheese[1]

- Boil 6 quarts of whole milk: In a large pot, bring the milk to boil over medium heat, stirring every so often, so it doesn't stick to the bottom of the pot. Once it boils, immediately turn off the heat.
- Stir in 3/4 cup lemon juice and 2 tablespoons of white vinegar using a spatula or slotted spoon. After about 5 minutes, the milk will begin to curdle.
- Strain the mixture with a fine-mesh strainer and a cheesecloth. After pouring the mixture through, pick up the cheesecloth and twist the top like a purse. Next, drain out as much of the whey as you can.
- Press the cheese by placing it onto a plate with a heavy pot or pan on top. You can leave it like this at room temperature overnight.
- Transfer the cheese to an airtight container the following day, and then use it as you wish.

Medium - Mozzarella[2]

- Crush 1/4 tablet of rennet and dissolve in 1/4 cup of cool water, or add 1/4 tsp single-strength liquid rennet to the water. Set your rennet mixture aside for later.
- Add 1 1/2 tsp of citric acid to 1 cup of cool water in a large pot.
- Pour cold full-fat milk into your pot and mix well with the citric acid.
- Heat the milk slowly to 90°F. As you approach 90°F, you may notice your milk curling slightly due to acidity and temperature.
- At 90°F, remove the pot from the burner and slowly add your rennet mixture. Stir in a top to bottom motion for approx. Thirty seconds, then stop and leave undisturbed for 5 minutes.
- After 5 minutes, it should look like custard, with separation between the curds and whey. If the curd is soft or the whey is milky, let it set longer, up to 30 more minutes.
- Cut the curds into 1" cubes.
- Place the pot back on the stove and heat to 105°F while slowly stirring the curds with your ladle.
- Take the pot off the burner and continue stirring slowly for 2-5 minutes—longer for a firmer cheese.
- Transfer the curds into a microwave-safe bowl and press the curd gently with your hand, pouring off as much whey as possible. You can keep the whey to use later in baking or as a soup stock.
- Add 1 tsp of salt to the curd and then microwave for 1 minute.
- Drain off any additional whey, then work the cheese with your hands.
- Microwave two more times for 30 seconds each, and repeat the kneading as in the last step to aid in more whey drain off and ensure even heating of the curds.
- Knead the curd similarly to bread dough until it is smooth and shiny. The cheese should be soft and pliable enough to stretch.

- Now knead your cheese back into a big ball, and as soon as it's cool enough to eat, you can give it a taste.

Hard - Parmesan

Unfortunately, most of us don't have the time, space, or ingredients to make homemade parmesan cheese. But if you've mastered some simpler types, why not try this recipe: https://cheesemaking.com/products/parmesan-style-cheese-making-recipe. You're going to need:

- Thermometer
- Curd Knife
- Slotted Ladle
- Cheesecloth
- Large Colander
- Medium Hard Cheese Mold
- Cheese Press

And up to a year of patience to properly age it. Good luck!

SOUTHWEST

ARIZONA

Uncovering secrets and hidden knowledge is the theme for the unique hobbies of Arizona.

COIN SHOOTING

Metal detecting is popular in Arizona, mainly because the geology makes it a great spot to find gold nuggets. But you don't need to try and strike it rich in a modern-day gold rush to enjoy this hobby. Since most of us don't live near gold veins or deposits, the rest of us can look for other hidden treasures.

Coin shooting is a specific type of metal detecting and targets finding historical coins. Since you have a specific object in mind to look for, you won't just be wandering around aimlessly on beaches hoping to find metal scraps. Instead, you'll need to research and target specific areas of historical importance to find the coins you are looking for. In fact, this research could be a hobby in and of itself.

While some specialized equipment is necessary, most entry-level metal detectors for beginner hobbyists are reasonably priced and can detect coin-sized objects. Look for a VLF (very-low-frequency) metal detector that fits your budget, is an appropriate size, and is recommended by other hobbyists.

A word of caution, though, disturbing historical sites and archeological artifacts may require specific permissions in your state. Make sure to contact some local metal-detecting groups so you are aware of all the local rules, and make some new friends!

The different sides of this hobby, researching potential coin locations, getting out there and detecting the coins, and finally deciding how to best display your finds keep coin shooting interesting; there's always something different to do.

ONLINE LEARNING

The best way to keep your mind sharp and stave off dementia and other cognitive issues associated with aging is to continue challenging your brain and constantly learning new things. Many people decide that retirement is the time to give themselves a much-needed break from the daily mental workouts of their careers. While taking some time off to recharge is a great idea, don't let your gray matter get too comfortable.

Arizona State University is known for its online education program and partnership with edX, a massive online education program open to anyone, with university-level courses developed by Harvard and MIT. But don't let those names intimidate you; no matter your level of education, interest, or enthusiasm, you can find online learning you will enjoy.

All you need is a computer and enough electronic know-how to sign yourself up and get videos started. You can watch classes on your phone if that's all you have available. Some courses might have reading material, others might be recorded talks or lectures, or you might sign up for something with live classes taught in real-time where you can ask the experts questions directly.

Pick up that favorite subject you never pursued as a career but always dreamed about, try some brain games or puzzles and challenge some friends and family members, or maybe you remember a documentary you enjoyed and want to learn more about. Don't think of this like going back to school; the choice is yours what you learn, how deep into the subject matter you dive, and if you start finding something boring, you can move on to a new topic to explore.

Whether you join a local college, community center, online program, or find a group of interested people at the local library, this can be a fulfilling and engaging way to keep your mind healthy long into retirement. Remember, use it or lose it!

COLORADO

Known for mountain communities and free-spiritedness, Colorado has a thriving economy and is a popular tourist destination. But while it may seem modern and wealthy compared to most other states, it is also home to traditional hobbies.

BOOK-BINDING

Many trades and crafts, made obsolete by the progress of technology, have managed to survive as hobbies. The American Academy of Bookbinding was founded in Telluride, Colorado, to create a place for people who care about the art of making books.

Traditional bookbinding by hand involves combining the individual sheets of paper into groups called 'signatures,' then sewing groups of these signatures together on one side to form the book's inside. After attaching a stiff outer layer and adding a cover design, the book is completed. Depending on the size and type of the book and the available equipment, there are many ways to bind a book and find the style that best suits you.

Bookbinding has undergone many changes throughout history, and the various methods have different levels of complexity, requirements for tools and materials, and necessary skill or dexterity. Nevertheless, with some research, you can learn how to create your own hand-bound masterpieces or even repair some treasured books.

If books aren't your thing, many traditional and artisan trades are on the verge of being lost to time but are being kept alive by passionate hobbyists looking for people to join in on the fun.

SPORT SHOOTING

Guns have a long history in the USA, and regardless of your opinion on them, they have established their place in America's past and present. Today, USA Shooting, headquartered in Colorado Springs, supports and trains Olympic and Paralympic athletes in several target shooting disciplines.

A test of coordination, eyesight, and nerves, target shooting has been popular since America's colonial era. However, there are many different disciplines, and most can use air guns if you don't feel comfortable handling more dangerous firearms.

You could try target shooting with pistols or rifles, trap shooting, or if your physical abilities aren't what they used to be, you could try bench rest, where the shooter sits in a chair with the gun supported by a table.

Shooting ranges are common in most areas of the USA, and there are an estimated 16,000 indoor ranges across America. This offers an excellent opportunity to test your skill against your previous best or in friendly competition with others. Who knows, maybe you'll have a knack for it and become a 'senior' Olympian.

NEW MEXICO

Hovering in the air and seemingly defying the laws of physics, the hobbies of New Mexico are mesmerizing and a bit mysterious.

SPOTTING UFOS

Some people like taking their fun seriously, learning valuable life skills, keeping their body and mind sharp, or creating works of art as their legacy to future generations. And others know that sometimes it's more about the journey than the destination.

I don't know if any UFO researchers have found anything, but if you go into this hobby with the right attitude, it can be a life-changing and fulfilling experience. It's not about discovering if there is life beyond this planet that has visited us; it's about enjoying the search and imagining the possibilities.

While Roswell, New Mexico, is home to the most famous UFO sighting, where the US government briefly announced the capture of a flying saucer in 1947 before confirming it was just a weather balloon, there are other sites across the US where UFO sightings are common. Reading about the history of unidentified flying objects, aliens, and the myths surrounding them can be fascinating, and doing your own UFO searching with a telescope or traveling to a common UFO sighting area can make an exciting travel itinerary.

Tracking the paranormal, whether UFOs, ghosts, or cryptids (animals that have never been proven to exist), can be an interesting hobby, as long as you don't go setting your hopes on actually finding anything.

FEEDING HUMMINGBIRDS

Did you know there are over 350 species of a hummingbird? While most of them live in South America, several species migrate north to the USA in the warmer months, and most pass through New Mexico. However, hummingbirds can be found in almost every state, depending on the time of year.

Putting up a hummingbird feeder or adding some nectar-rich flowers to your garden is an easy way to attract hummingbirds, and many people enjoy watching the antics of these amazing birds. While you can't keep a hummingbird as a pet (it's illegal in the USA), making sure there are some high-calorie snacks available for them after their long migration from South America is encouraged and helps keep their populations strong.

To get you started with your new hobby, here are some fun facts and hummingbird behaviors you could watch for:

- A hummingbird's sound comes from its wings, beating more than 50 times a second. But hummingbirds can make other sounds; try to listen for a thrumming or chirping sound made by the males' tail feathers as they dive to impress the female.
- Hummingbirds can hover, fly backward, and even upside-down. See if you can capture this in a picture or on video.
- Many male hummingbirds have iridescent feathers that they will show off during mating displays. They often angle

themselves so a perched female will see the sun reflecting off their feathers; you can use this to find the best spots to take their pictures.
- Nests are tiny, often smaller than a golf ball, and very well camouflaged. If you notice female hummingbirds making trips around your yard, pull out binoculars and try to spot one!

Suppose you want to take things a little more seriously and contribute to science. In that case, you could join a hummingbird tracking group, which notes the dates of each species of hummingbird's annual migration and helps scientists track their population numbers.

OKLAHOMA

You have a lifetime of experience, but have you taken a chance and expressed yourself yet? Maybe retirement is the time to jump out of your shell and share your talents with everyone around you. The hobbies from Oklahoma will give you the tools and confidence you need to put yourself out there.

FOLK MUSIC

American folk music only began coming into the public eye after the Great Depression. Folk festivals began to gain popularity as these difficult times sparked multiple political and social movements. Woody Guthrie was an Oklahoman native and one of the most influential figures in American folk music. You've probably heard *'This Land is Your Land'* and many other songs of his without ever knowing who the original artist was.

Every region in America has its own history and style of folk music. Learning about and listening to folk music is a great way to explore your heritage and history. Many of the most famous folk songs remain part of our culture, passed on and changed over time, continuing to spread their messages.

So you could either become a folk music connoisseur, pick your favorite style and become more familiar with its origins and most prominent singers, and discover how it has influenced today's music and even politics. Or you could start learning to play and sing some of these songs. Classic American folk songs are designed for sing-alongs, so this can be a fun activity, and if you're the person who can lead the music and teach others the words, that would be a rewarding hobby.

If you're feeling even more ambitious, you could try your hand at writing a new folk song in the style of your choice. Modern American folk music has its unique style, but it takes passionate people like you to keep these traditions alive and well.

MUSICAL THEATER

Oklahoma!, a Rodgers and Hammerstein Broadway hit from the 1940s, is one of the classics of American musical theater. Musical theater, or musicals, are like the modern version of opera, with acting, singing, dancing, and most importantly, in English. Of course, if you fancy yourself a pro on the stage, you shouldn't have a problem finding a local or community theater group to join. But there are many other ways to be a part of the experience, even if you have severe stage fright.

Musical productions need all kinds of volunteers and support to get the show ready for opening night.

Directors, choreographers, and musicians all help with the creative process from behind the scenes. Props, costumes, sets, and lighting must be implemented with some technical know-how and elbow grease. There are also jobs like producing, fundraising and finance, marketing, and casting agents that build the foundation for the show to happen. Or you could work in the box office, as an usher, or selling refreshments so you can be there on opening night. There will be some way for you to contribute, where you can use some of your skills to be a part of the show's success.

Here are some of the most popular American musicals for amateur theater. Do any of these suit your taste?

- Oklahoma!
- The Sound of Music
- Guys and Dolls
- Little Shop of Horrors
- Mamma Mia
- Grease
- The Wizard of Oz

TEXAS

Texas is a handful and sometimes seems like its own country within the USA. So it only makes sense that we'll be working with our hands to take on the hobbies of Texas.

SKIPPING STONES

A little competition can turn any simple everyday activity into a hobby, and what could be simpler than skipping stones? Head down to the nearest creek, lake, or beach, find a smooth flat stone that fits nicely into the palm of your hand, and try to make it bounce across the water surface as many times as you can. There isn't much to it, but adding that dash of competition might be just what you need to turn this into a hobby.

The North American Stone Skipping Association (NASSA) was founded in 1989 in Driftwood, Texas. The NASSA world championships were held in Texas until 1992 when they started moving around to different international locations.

The current world record is 88 skips, but anything over 20 skips is a good score in a competition. Here are some tips:

- Find a flat, oval stone that fits comfortably in the palm of your hand.
- Hold the stone with your forefinger and thumb so that you can spin it to your throw. This adds a gyroscopic effect that keeps the stone stable during its flight.
- Try to have the stone hit the water at an angle between 10 and 20 degrees.
- Speed is essential; the stone needs to move fairly quickly to skip, and each skip will slow it down.

Try experimenting with different techniques and types of stone. Maybe you aren't as limber and need more of an underhand throw. Perhaps you have better luck with slightly rougher stones. And if you're worried that you have lost your throwing strength in retirement, remember that in Japanese skimming contests, the best throws are not only judged on the number of skips and distance traveled but by their aesthetic qualities. Why not record some of your throws in scenic locations, with dramatic arcs as your throw travels over an undisturbed lake surface.

LEATHER PYROGRAPHY

Pyrography is a lesser-known art form created by burning objects by hand with burners or hot pokers. Also called wood burning or pokerwork, the distinctive style of this art form has an old-west feel. Most pyrography is done on wood, with the grain, texture, and color giving a different style and acting as the canvas for the pyrography. But another option for aspiring pyrographic artists is to work with leather. Texas is famous for its cattle ranches, making it a great place to try your hand at burning images into a leather canvas.

Similar to other monochromatic art mediums like charcoal, pencil sketches, or black and white photography, it takes a lot of creativity and skill to make the pyrography art pop. Also, leather tends to be easier to work with than wood, as it allows for more subtle shading. Either way, ensure that whatever material you work with hasn't been chemically treated. This means you'll need to find vegetable-tanned leather instead of the standard chemically-tanned stuff.

You could go for a rustic approach and try to craft images with a red-hot poker, but it would probably be easier to invest in a woodburning pen. Woodburning kits will work on leather, although you might need to spend some time experimenting with different heat settings. Just like watercolors, it can be challenging to salvage mistakes, so this is definitely a hobby for the patient and precise.

Example of pyrography on wood[1]

UTAH

Utah is known for many things, its beautiful snow, impressive natural parks, and of course, fry sauce. Let's look at two hobbies you have probably heard of but might not have gotten around to trying.

STARGAZING

One of the defining characteristics of the American landscape is the wide open spaces, with clear blue skies and untouched wilderness for miles around. But these wide open spaces become even more spectacular at night.

While many of us are stuck in cities where the lights from shops, skyscrapers, and suburbs wash out the night sky, there are still many parts of our country where you can get a good look at the stars. A few of the best spots for stargazing are in Utah. For example, Bryce Canyon National Park has an astronomy program with 'dark rangers' to help tourists enjoy the evening. The town of Torrey put in place outdoor lighting rules to enhance their nighttime views and those in the nearby Capitol Reef National Park.

If you aren't near Utah and have been missing seeing the stars, here are a few tips to find the perfect night scenery:

- Avoid urban areas and bright lights; even going a few minutes outside of the city can drastically improve the view
- Spots at higher elevations are generally better; even just the top of a hill can work; the best spots will have an unobstructed view that stretches to the horizon
- Stars look brighter on days when the air is clear, dry, and clean, so you can always take a look at the weather forecast and local air quality index to plan things in advance
- It also couldn't hurt to see if there is a local astronomy club to get some local tips

Even if astronomy and telescopes aren't your things, anyone can learn to pick out a few constellations, watch for shooting stars, or appreciate a quiet starlit evening. If you're looking for a little more, you could try spotting planets (with a telescope), try to get the best view of the Milky way, enjoy the Northern Lights, or catch a meteor shower.

A starry night[1]

TABLETOP GAMES

Where are you the most likely to find a group of people sitting around engaging in the world's most famous tabletop role-playing game,

Dungeons, and Dragons? The answer is the state of Utah; who would have guessed. Most people have probably heard of this tabletop role-playing game, but how many of us have tried it?

While mental images of awkward teenagers talking about wizards and goblins might make this hobby a bit off-putting for some, let's take a deeper look at the variety of tabletop games available today. They are a great way to get people together for a social activity that is more about telling a creative group story than rolling dice and pretending to slay trolls. Here are examples of different types of more modern and accessible tabletop games.

Fiasco

A game for 3 to 5 people is about playing out disastrous situations and is designed as a collaborative storytelling experience. Games last an hour or two and consist of plans constantly going wrong and poor decisions, all with the backdrop of a black-comedy caper movie.

Forbidden Island

This game is all about cooperation, not competition. All the players will work together to try and solve the mysteries of the Forbidden Island, emphasizing teamwork and communication. This can be a little more complicated, but it can still be fun for new players since you're all working together.

Sheriff of Nottingham

This is a 'social deduction' game, also described as a session of competitive dishonesty. The players will bluff and deceive each other as they try to smuggle goods past the sheriff. These games can bring out your social group's ruthless and cunning sides and never play out the same way twice.

WEST COAST

ALASKA

Alaska is America's northern frontier. Untamed wilderness with only small remote cities makes this a paradise for outdoor hobbies and exploring nature. But you don't have to travel to the ends of Alaska to find the wilderness in America.

SNOWSHOEING

Snowshoes are a surprisingly ancient technology, thought to have originated thousands of years ago, maybe mimicking the large feet of the aptly named snowshoe hare. Almost all of North America's Indigenous people developed some form of the snowshoe to help them stay mobile in the winter season.

Snowshoes spread out your weight over a large area, so anyone can easily traverse over deep snow without falling in or getting stuck. Anyone can learn the basics in about an hour, although it might take a few weeks to feel completely comfortable. Before you know it, you will be breaking new trails (making new tracks in fresh snow) and leading your group on a crisp wilderness hike.

Although they might seem simple to use, there are some basic techniques for using snowshoes[1]:

- **Walking** - snowshoes are often wide enough that trying to walk without stepping on your own feet can be exhausting. Instead, remember to slide the snowshoes over each other so you can keep your stride to its regular width.
- **Turning** - tight turns can be tricky, and beginner snowshoers often have to travel in a semi-circle motion to change direction. A more advanced move is to use a kick-turn, similar to traditional skiing.
- **Uphill** - it can be helpful to kick into the snow to create small steps for stability and stamp them down to make them secure. While the fastest way up a hill is to point yourself right at the top, you can always make a zig-zag 'switchback' pattern if things feel too steep.
- **Downhill** - Keep your shoe level with the horizon on a slight slope. But as things get steeper, you may have to turn and sidestep down hills. If the coast is clear, you can try glissading: put your weight on your heels, pull up your toes, and slide-step down the hill. You can also slide down on your backside if you need a well-deserved break after climbing a large hill!
- **Getting up** - Nobody is an expert immediately, so chances are you will take a fall while learning (and hopefully have that fall broken by some fluffy snow). Just remember to roll onto your front, put one knee up and push into a half kneeling position, then use a pole or hiking staff for support and push yourself back up.

If snowshoeing isn't your thing, many other ways of getting around in the great outdoors can be fun hobbies that challenge you mentally and physically. Cross-country skiing and sledding, or if you live in a warmer climate, you could even consider roller-blading or skateboarding (although the falls while learning these can be more painful.) Whatever you choose, finding a way to add excitement and challenge to a regular walk is a great way to keep life fresh and exciting.

DOG TRAINING

Whether or not you have your own furry four-legged friend, learning how to relate to and train animals can be extremely rewarding.

One of the most extreme examples of dog training is the Iditarod, an annual dog sled race from Anchorage to Nome, crossing most of Alaska. Involving teams of a dozen or more dogs traveling for two weeks under extreme weather conditions in dangerous terrain, the dogs must be intensely trained and in perfect physical condition.

While training a long-distance arctic dog-sled team is probably more of a challenge than most of us would be up for in retirement, there are plenty of simple things you can train your pets to do that can make your life easier and their life more exciting.

There are many different styles of dog training, and the philosophies behind the best ways to train animals have changed over the years. What has remained the same is that dogs are intelligent animals and can learn in various ways through positive reinforcement, repetitive actions, observation, or even inference.

The basic obedience commands, learning to come, sit, stay, heel, off, and not bark at or jump up on everybody, are all pretty straightforward and things most dogs can learn to do, but why not give your best friend some extra skills to stand out at the dog park.

You could start with the classics, like shaking hands, playing dead, and rolling over, or maybe add some fun variations like 'spin around.' A neat trick is to train your dog to react to a few non-verbal commands, so you can say whatever you want while your furry friend astounds strangers at the park. More complicated obedience commands like 'watch' or 'touch' can also benefit your relationship with your pet.

Other animals can also learn basic commands (yes, cats!), and even if you don't have a pet, understanding how pets think and learn can make interacting with animals more enjoyable.

CALIFORNIA

In the home of Hollywood, the hobbies are all about getting up on the stage. Don't worry; it's much easier than it sounds.

ACTING AS AN EXTRA

While starting a new career as an actor or actress during retirement might be a long-shot, if your only goal is to make it onto the big screen, there are some options. Even if you don't live near Hollywood, there are probably movies, T.V. shows, or maybe even local news filming somewhere near you. Becoming a background character, or 'extra,' can be a fun hobby and an exciting way to learn about how media is made.

Here are a few ways to become an extra:

- Be on the lookout for casting calls and ready to respond with a clear photo, contact info, and an (accurate) physical description of yourself. You'll need to look around in your local paper or online for what productions are filming near you; many have production websites or social media pages. You can

- also check with your city or state to see if they have a film office.
- Register with a casting agency or two, this shouldn't cost money upfront, but they might take a small part of any payments you receive.

Make sure you follow all the instructions (for instance, specific clothing,) show up on time, behave professionally, and be prepared for a lot of standing around and waiting.

Being an extra isn't necessarily the most exciting hobby minute-to-minute. Still, unless you're retiring from an entertainment career, it might be the easiest way to show up in a theater near you and brag about 'starring' in the latest movies.

POETRY SLAMS

Poetry has a reputation for being a bit boring and stuffy. But America has found a way to liven things up a little. In the 1980s, poetry slams became popular in Chicago and San Francisco. Spoken word poetry is performed live in front of an audience and usually a panel of judges. With roots in hip-hop music, poetry slams often have cheering, audience participation, and much more personality than a traditional poetry reading.

The first National Poetry Slam took place in San Francisco in 1990, and similar events have been slowly growing and spreading around the globe ever since.

So what does it take to compete in a local poetry slam?

Many slams are 'open,' so anyone can sign up while there are still slots available. So you're ready to go if you can find a local club or theater with an open poetry slam!

Poets typically perform in up to three rounds, with a time limit of three minutes per poem. So you will need to have some material prepped, but not that much. The style of your poetry is all up to you. Rhyming or not, delivered as a rant or a rap, comedic or serious, everything is accepted. What is popular is constantly changing over time and between regions, so whatever style you have may or may not be in vogue. The only constant rule is that you need to win over the audience!

Just bring your poems since props, costumes, and background music are not allowed. Of course, you'll also need a pretty hefty dose of confidence, but maybe this is just the hobby to help build yourself up.

HAWAII

One of the most unique cultures within a country full of unique cultures. There is a lot to discover from the Hawaiian people, and these next two hobbies will only begin to scratch the surface.

UKULELE

For those of us that were, how should we say, less musically inclined earlier in life, it might seem impossible to master an instrument in retirement. Learning to read music, taking lessons, the endless scales, and practice doesn't sound like most people's retirement dream.

But not every instrument requires years of grueling practice.

The ukulele is one of the easiest instruments to learn, but you can still spend a lifetime improving. While you won't be a ukulele expert right away, many absolute musical beginners find themselves able to play a song or two after just a few weeks, and it is one of the most common instruments for self-teaching.

There are only four strings, and most music is written with chord charts that show the exact positions of your fingers on the strings. Practice a few chords, learn to hold the ukulele and some basic strumming patterns, and you're off!

Playing a few chords while you (or someone else) sings along at home or on a Hawaiian beach and being able to finally join in on those family sing-alongs you have been missing out on is the perfect retirement activity.

And don't worry if you get stuck, ukulele video tutorials are very popular on YouTube and in free apps, so it won't be hard to find a bit of free instruction if you need it. Here are some popular beginner ukulele songs to try out:

- "Brown Eyed Girl" – Van Morrison
- "Someone Like You" – Adele
- "Have You Ever Seen The Rain?" – Creedence Clearwater Revival
- "I'm Yours" – Jason Mraz
- "Sweet Home Alabama" – Lynyrd Skynyrd
- "Let It Be" – The Beatles
- "Hallelujah" – Leonard Cohen

And, of course, the Hawaiian favorite...

- "Somewhere Over The Rainbow" – Israel Kamakawiwo'ole

HULA

The hula is a traditional Hawaiian dance, and while many of us can probably do a quick imitation of the hula for fun on the beach, there is a lot more to this dance than you might think.

First, the hula is meant to accompany a song or a chant, with the dance moves representing the story being told. There is a wide range of styles, going back hundreds of years and representing ancient traditions, myths, and legends, to more modern styles influenced by Western culture that resemble today's popular music.

Although it may not be easy to find a traditional hula instructor where you live, called a *Kumu hula*, you can always get started by following along with some videos or online instructions. Who knows, countless people across America are eager to share their culture and spread their traditions to new people.

If you're getting up there in years and thinking that dance might be beyond your physical abilities, some hula dances (called *NoHo dances*) are performed from a sitting position. Remember, it's not about how fast or energetic you are; the hula is a way to tell stories through deliberate and refined body movements. There are many hand and arm movements you can focus on, allowing you to put on an impressive and emotional performance without having to worry too much about moving your feet and hips.

IDAHO

Many people make the mistake of trying to get into overly elaborate, complicated, and expensive hobbies when they retire. We all know that sometimes it's better to keep things simple, and that's what we're going to try with these hobbies from Idaho.

GOING GREEN

We hear the warnings all the time about toxic chemicals all around us and how there are many benefits to ourselves and others if we could 'go green.' Many of us would like to make the right choice for the environment (and ourselves), but those green products are often expensive to buy or difficult and time-consuming to make ourselves.

To get you over that hurdle, here are some quick and easy recipes for green products that can be used to make sure the world lasts for the next generation, or as Idahoans might say, '*Esto Perpetua.*'

Making safe household products for yourself, family, and friends can be a rewarding hobby that also makes the world a better place. And in the spirit of Idaho, these are all made from potatoes!

Rust Remover

- Cut a potato in half, in whichever way is easier to hold in your hand
- Dip the cut end into a strong baking soda solution
- Rub the cut end over any rusty areas; the oxalic acid from the potato mixed with the baking soda will dissolve that rust
- If the potato gets slippery, cut a slice off the end and reapply baking soda
- Once the rust is removed, rinse and dry
- Works on cast iron, knives, or even tarnished silverware

Defogger

- Rub lenses, glass, or windows with a cut potato
- This will leave some starch on the surface, which prevents fog build-up

Stain Remover

- Cut a slice of potato
- Rub against stained material or hands
- Works best against berry or fruit stains (including wine)

Remove or clean up broken glass

- Cut a potato in half (do you see a pattern here?)
- Press the cut side of the potato into the broken glass
- Also works for broken light bulbs that are stuck in their sockets

LAUGHING CLUBS

The town of Pocatello is tucked away in the southeast corner of Idaho. While this idyllic community experiences pleasant warm summers, it can also experience some harsh winter weather. After a particularly bad winter in 1948, the mayor at the time passed the 'smile ordinance[1],' which made it illegal not to smile. Although the law isn't enforced and was mostly forgotten until the 1980s, the city now has an annual event called 'smile days,' with contests, parades, and fake arrests for frowning people who don't play along. But Pocatello isn't the only place Americans are smiling.

Laughing clubs are groups of people who get together and use laughter as a form of exercise. Also called laughing yoga, all you need is a space ample enough for everyone (inside or outside) and one that preferably doesn't echo too much. There are many health benefits to getting a weekly dose of laughing out loud, and it can be just what the doctor ordered to keep a positive mindset as you transition into retirement or other life changes. Here are a few of the purported health benefits of regular laughter[2]:

- Eases muscle tension
- Lowers stress
- Releases dopamine and endorphins
- Increases blood circulation
- Boosts immunity
- Reduces risk of heart disease, and
- Helps promote lower blood sugar levels

MONTANA

Controlling things that fly through the air is the theme behind the hobbies of Montana. Just watch your aim and try not to crash into anything.

DISC GOLF

Everyone is likely familiar with golf, and it is popular for a reason. A good choice, yes, but it would be hard to consider golf a unique hobby.

What if you added a twist and played with a frisbee instead? No expensive clubs to lug around, a more relaxed atmosphere, and a new type of challenge to revitalize your mind and body.

Disc golf is a global sport, but America has over three-quarters of the courses worldwide, with 6,652 disc courses spread across the USA.

One of the most famous courses is Diamond X, near Billings, Montana. Not only is it one of the most challenging disc golf courses in the world, but the record for the longest ace (disc golf's version of a hole-in-one) was also set there in 2002, at a distance of 726 feet.

So what exactly are the rules of disc golf?

Just like traditional golf, the objective is to reach the hole in the fewest possible plays, and each throw (and penalty) counts for one.

Each hole begins with a tee throw from within a designated area. Each subsequent throw is from a spot just behind where the disc landed. You are allowed a running start if you are more than 30 feet from the target, but if you are within that distance, you must be balanced on two feet.

Instead of a hole, disc golf uses a chain basket, and the hole is completed when the disc lands in the basket or if it gets suspended within the basket's chains.

If you have a poor throw and end up outside the marked boundaries, you are out-of-bounds, and you must play your next throw from the point where your disc crossed the boundary. Disc golf courses are often in public parks, and other park users are always given the right-of-way.

The same general rules of courtesy and etiquette as traditional golf apply, and if you start getting serious, you can get specialized long-range, short-range, and 'putting' discs to improve your game.

DRONE PHOTOGRAPHY

Almost everyone you know has a camera that would shame the technology of a few decades ago. There are also enough automatic assists and touch-up tools freely available that almost everyone you know is also taking pretty good pictures. Having photography as a hobby doesn't seem all that worthwhile or impressive anymore, now that it has become so easy.

So why not make things a little more challenging?

One of the best places to fly drones in the USA is Bitterroot Valley, Montana. Wide-open spaces surrounded by rolling hills and carpeted with vibrant forests make this the perfect place to practice your flying and your camera work. Even a simple photo shot straight down from a drone high above onto a natural feature or cityscape can be very impressive, but it's going to take a little work to get there.

First, you'll need to purchase a drone. An entry-level one capable of taking pictures has become much more affordable recently, but be prepared to spend a few hundred dollars.

Next up, you have to learn to fly. Controlling a drone has gotten relatively straightforward, but the more challenging part is doing it safely and legally. Making sure you avoid obstacles, don't damage any structures, avoid invading people's privacy, and follow local and federal aircraft regulations will take a bit of research. Luckily you don't have to be a pioneer here and can start by joining a local drone group or getting the basics from the experts online.

Finally, you'll have to line up that perfect shot.

In the early days of photography and until digital cameras replaced film, photography was almost a sport. Finding the perfect spot, with the ideal light, getting your settings just right, all with limited chances to capture that moment based on what was remaining on your roll of film. Drone photography will recapture that element of excitement. Thinking outside the box to imagine what overhead perspectives will be most impressive, deftly piloting your drone through all of the physical (and legal) obstacles, and capturing that moment at the perfect height, the ideal time, and before your batteries run out and you have to head back to the ground.

So let's bring some skill and effort back into photography and make this classic hobby feel rewarding again.

NEVADA

There is more to Nevada than the city of Las Vegas, rugged mountains, hot sandy deserts, Hoover dam, Lake Tahoe, silver mines, and even Area 51. But unfortunately, the allure of the Las Vegas Strip was too much to resist, and the hobbies here are all in the cards.

CARD GAMES

Nevada is home to the city of Las Vegas, known around the world for its gambling and entertainment. While I wouldn't necessarily recommend poker or blackjack as great ways to spend a large part of your time in retirement, many lesser-known card games can be just as thrilling. Here are a few examples that use a standard 52-card deck; maybe you have heard of some before, and perhaps some are new to you and worth trying.

Accordion Solitaire - for one person. One of the more difficult solitaire games, with plenty of ways to plan your strategy since you can see all the cards from the start. Begin with all 52 cards in a single row, then gradually compress the row by stacking the cards according to the rules. The game is won when all the cards are in one stack.

Skitgubbe - for 2 to 4 people. This two-phase game starts similar to War, gradually building up the players' hands, and then in the second phase switches to a rummy-style game where the players have to discard that same hand. The Skitgubbe (dirty old man)[1] is the last player to go out.

Sheepshead - for 2 to 8 people (best with 5). Based on a Bavarian trick-taking card game, there are many American variations for different amounts of people, including teams or pairs. Usually, the 2 through 6 cards of all four suits are removed, and the remaining cards are assigned a score. There are offensive and defensive roles, complex strategies, and it might take years to master the game. If you are looking for an alternative to bridge or euchre, give this a try!

Tycoon - for 3 to 8 people. At the beginning of the round, each player is assigned a role with a title (like a millionaire, commoner, or pauper) based on their performance in the previous round. Every region has its favorite titles, so feel free to come up with your own. According to the rules, the goal is to remove cards from your hand as quickly as possible, with the fastest player receiving the best title and the slowest the worst. The game may also get more complicated as more rounds are played, as a common house rule is that the winner of the last round is allowed to add (or remove) a new rule to the game. This can make for an interesting social element that makes the game fresh whenever you play with new people.

MAGIC TRICKS

Pick a card, any card. While spouting that off without prompting might earn you a few groans and eye rolls at a party, there is a reason magic has been a popular hobby for thousands of years.

Magic tricks don't have to be corny or cheesy, and a big part of the creativity in this hobby is how you present yourself. People love to be fooled and amazed; you must find the right time, place, and style. So if you start learning magic, what are some basics you need to know?

First, there are many different types of magic. Stage magic or escape tricks involve large props, and maybe an assistant, close-up magic, and street magic are performed within arms reach of the audience with no room for error, relying on sleight-of-hand and offshoots like mentalism rely on observational skills or subtle psychological manipulation.

But while that is starting to sound complicated, there are only a handful of basic magic tricks. The difference from one magician to the next is mainly in the performance and narrative around the trick, with relatively minor alterations in the methods they use to fool the audience.

Here are the basics of magic[2]:

- Production - Making something appear out of nowhere (like a rabbit out of a hat)
- Vanishing - Making something disappear without a trace (like a ball under a cup)
- Transformation - Changing an object's form or properties (size, color, etc.) or turning it into something completely different (like a handkerchief into a dove)
- Restoration - Destroying or damaging an object then returning it to its previous undamaged state (like sawing a lady in half and putting her back together)
- Transportation - Make an object appear to move from one place to another
- Transposition or Double Transportation - Making multiple objects change places
- Escape - Breaking free from restraints such as locks, handcuffs, or a straight jacket (think Harry Houdini)
- Levitation - Making something or someone appear to defy gravity

- Penetration - Making a solid object appear to pass through another object
- Prediction - Predicting an outcome or an audience member's choice in advance (if you decide to go with picking a card, any card...)

OREGON

Oregon has a reputation for being a bit quirky and trendy. We're going to ride that wave of hipster energy to develop some interesting hobbies that will add some personality to your retirement.

HOME-BREWING KOMBUCHA

Kombucha is a fermented tea produced from a SCOBY (symbiotic culture of bacteria and yeast) and added flavorings. The SCOBY is alive and similar to a mother-dough used when making sourdough bread. Known for its probiotic benefits, kombucha has been gaining popularity across the USA since the late 1990s.

Oregon was home to some of the first kombucha brands, with small batch or home-brewed kombucha becoming extremely popular. Similar to making wines or beers, many flavors and techniques are involved, and no two kombuchas are the same.

Since kombucha is fermented, it can contain alcohol (usually less than 0.5%), but the intent is usually to reduce the alcohol content as much as possible in the finished product.

It is essential to brew kombucha correctly; improperly made fermented beverages can be dangerous if not produced correctly. But once you have a good grasp on the safety details, the actual brewing process is pretty simple. Here is a quick overview of the steps involved in making your own:

- Brew some tea with a flavor you like
- Add a SCOBY
- Let it sit for a week or more
- Remove the SCOBY
- Bottle it; you can add fruit juice, spices, or other flavors if you like

There you have it, much more straightforward than making your own beer or wine, and with some added health benefits.

KALEIDOSCOPES

What's a kaleidoscope? Aren't they those tube things kids used to play with the colors inside? As adults, they might seem boring but think back to when you were a child and could be mesmerized by something so simple. But how simple are they really? If I asked you how kaleidoscopes worked, would you be able to explain what is happening inside? Just read on, and in a few short paragraphs, you'll be an expert.

Kaleidoscopes are made by placing two or more mirrors at angles in a tube so that the objects viewed at the far end are displayed as symmetrical patterns due to repeated reflections. Rotating the tube in various ways changes the image, so the symmetrical image is continuously shifted before your eyes.

The science behind kaleidoscopes has been known since ancient times, but they didn't start to get impressive until a few advancements in the theory of optics were made in the last century. Over a million people annually see *'Kaleidoscopes: Reflections of Science and Art,'* an exhibit created by artist Thea Marshall and Eugene, Oregon's Willamette Science and Technology Center, which is definitely still popular.

Planning out how to place the mirrors and understanding how the reflections will look and transform the appearance of your colorful tube can be complicated or take a bit of patience and experimenting.

Here are some instructions to create a reasonably simple kaleidoscope; consider it your first practice try, and don't worry too much about how it turns out:

1. Get a cheap locker or bathroom mirror and cut it into three 1 ½" strips with a box cutter. Cheap mirrors aren't usually glass and are easy to cut safely.
2. Lay the three mirror strips side by side and upside down, and tape them together in a triangle shape (reflective sides in.)
3. Cut a cardboard tube to the length of your mirrors, with an extra 1/3" at the end.
4. Place one end of the cardboard tube flat on a piece of construction paper, and cut a triangle or circle in the center of the paper to view through. Tape your 'cap' to the tube with the hole centered.
5. Use an empty plastic container or two and trace two circles using the end of your tube. Draw around the previous ones with an object that's just slightly larger than your tube (like a cup). Then, cut around each of the circles to make some lenses.
6. Assemble the kaleidoscope by first sliding the triangular mirror inside the cardboard tube. Take the smaller lens and place it inside your tube against the edges of the mirror, forming a small pouch hanging into the tube at the far end across from your peephole. Place some beads, stones, or other colorful objects on top of the lens and use the second lens as a cap, taping it together inside the tube.

7. Decorate the outside of the tube however you like and enjoy the show.

Once you've practiced a few times, you can try using sturdier and more impressive materials to construct your kaleidoscopes. A similar illusion can be created with an 'infinity mirror,' which can create a stunning effect, and these are also reasonably simple to build and can be impressive art pieces.

WASHINGTON

Connecting and sharing with others in our retirement years is the theme for Washington, a beautiful west coast state with incredible access to nature and a thriving economy.

FARMERS MARKETS

Whether you're going to buy, sell, or just people-watch, farmer's markets and public markets are a great way to spend a day out. One of the USA's most famous farmer's markets is the Pike Place Market in Seattle, Washington.

You can get organic products directly from the person who grew or made them or discover what creations local artisans have dreamt up, and there is always something new to see. Stay for lunch, and even if you plan to go and pick up a bunch of fresh, healthy produce, there are usually more than a few delicious treats to be found too.

If you have another hobby of your own and want to show off or sell what you make, a farmer's market is the place to do it. Stalls are usually affordable and much less time-consuming than running your own shop. You also chat with the regulars and meet people who appreciate your talents.

Try making a hobby of traveling around your area and finding your favorite markets. Maybe there are some specialty things you can't find anywhere else or artisan products you have never heard of before. Use this time to get inspiration or revitalize your creativity.

Pike Place Market, Seattle[1]

DIGITAL LIBRARIES

There is nothing quite like going to the public library. Faced with shelves upon shelves of books, knowing that you could take any of them home with you, and realizing that the possibilities are almost endless. Just like everything else today, there are also online versions of libraries.

Project Gutenberg, founded by Washington State native Michael S. Hart, was the first digital library. Starting with a copy of the United States Declaration of Independence, it has grown to include over 50,000 ebooks in the public domain and, therefore, are free to download, share, and read at your leisure. That should be enough to sustain even the fastest reader for a lifetime.

You could try turning this into a bona fide hobby by starting your own digital book club. One of the trickiest parts about starting a book club or a similar meet-up group is that people get busy or distracted, and as soon as it becomes a little bit difficult, they begin to make excuses. Before you know it, your healthily populated book club is losing members and motivation, becoming more of a chore than a hobby. With a digital book club, nobody has to worry about tracking down copies or buying books online since everything is available, easy to find, and free to use and share. Making things easier typically makes things more fun.

Another thing you could try is volunteer reading. Most volunteer reading groups focus on helping children learn to read, and there aren't many things more satisfying than helping someone decipher their first book. While traditionally, volunteer readers had to come to schools to do this work, nowadays, you can find ways to become a volunteer reader online. Working your way through a digital library and having your 'student' pick out their first books would be a rewarding way to spend some of your retirement.

WYOMING

Mountain ranges and sparsely populated plains exemplify Wyoming, the state with the least amount of people and the lowest population density. You might feel like you've traveled back to the wild west. So let's put on our cowboy hats and giddy up.

NATIONAL PARKS

It may surprise some people that the United States invented the idea of a national park. Despite America's relatively young age compared to the countries of Europe and Asia, the idea of a public park for the benefit and enjoyment of all of the people of the land was something completely new.

Yellowstone National Park is the first and arguably most famous national park. Situated in Wyoming (but extending slightly into Montana and Idaho), it is known for its geological features like the geyser Old Faithful and its plentiful wildlife. But with 59 National parks in the USA, there are probably one or two not far from where you live.

Visiting different national parks or getting to know your nearest parks can be a fulfilling hobby. Learning about natural history and wildlife and always asking the park ranger what their favorite things to do and see are is always a good idea.

Here are a few suggestions to make sure your next experience in a National Park is worth the trip:

• Pick the right season - Ensure the park is open during the time of year when you want to go, as many parks are closed at certain times due to dangerous conditions, and some might be unpleasant depending on the time of year. Nobody needs to see Death Valley at the peak of the summer heat.

- Try staying at the lodge - Many national parks have their own dedicated lodges, full of history and conveniently located within the park. Just remember to plan ahead and book early.
- Do some planning - Always head out knowing what you want to see, where those things are, and how realistic it is to get around. National Parks can be huge, so a little planning can save you time and help you with proper packing.
- Get the app - Many parks have their own apps that give you basic history and information. Of course, also having a compass and GPS included doesn't hurt.
- Stay safe - Some basic, easy-to-follow rules will ensure you don't accidentally start a wildfire, get in trouble with wildlife, or otherwise cause any damage to these amazing areas. Always listen to warnings and advice from the park ranger, and bring a backup paper map.

FACIAL HAIR ART

An impressive horseshoe mustache is the trademark of any great cowboy. Add a cattleman hat and some boots, and you'll complete an iconic American look. While Hollywood cowboys may have been clean-shaven, the real deal would have impressive beards after spending weeks camping under the stars in the wilderness. Now that you're no longer stuck going into a stuffy office, it's time to let out your wild side and grow an impressive work of art on your face.

If your new mustache is turning out better than you expected, and your significant other is tolerating it, maybe you could even enter a mustache or beard competition. The National Beard and Moustache Championships involve elaborate designs; who knows; maybe you could be a world champion one day[1]. Judging occurs across a dozen or more styles, so whether you are best suited to growing a Hungarian, Fu Manchu, or full beard, there will be a perfect category for you.

Sorry ladies, this hobby is only for retired men, but that doesn't mean you can't try and adapt this for yourself. How long have you suffered a conservative 'normal' hairstyle just to fit in and look presentable for your job? Now is your chance to pick any style or color and express yourself.

Remember, this time of your life is for you, so stop worrying about what others think and display your face and hairstyle like the masterpiece you know you are!

WASHINGTON D.C.

It might surprise you that the place with the highest increase in marriage rates across America is the District of Columbia. But who is going to help all those new couples tie the knot?

You are!

WEDDING OFFICIATING

The last hobby on our journey around the USA is bringing new beginnings to others. Many couples without strong religious ties or looking for a more casual ceremony will ask friends or family members to officiate their wedding, adding a personal touch.

Suppose you get some experience with close relationships and good word of mouth. In that case, you can branch out, and you might find yourself getting requests to officiate the weddings of strangers, making your new hobby, possibly a small business. Becoming a wedding officiant can let you be a big part of their special day, helping them realize the perfect moment they've always dreamed of.

The legal requirements for becoming an officiant vary between states, and you will most likely have to register yourself. Additionally, many online churches and organizations are set up specifically to help people legally take on this role. Alternatively, many couples will do an official legal ceremony separately from their celebratory wedding ceremony with friends or family, and anyone can play the part of the officiant in those cases.

Officiants also don't just show up for the first time at the ceremony; they will often meet with the couple in advance to get an idea of what their personalities are like; they might help with designing the format and wording for the ceremony, crafting vows, or adding any customized touches while ensuring all of the legal requirements are still met. It's quite a creative process.

It might sound a bit stressful, but once you've done it once or twice, you'll realize that your part, while important, is pretty small. So if you love weddings, dressing up in official-looking outfits, and briefly being the center of attention (or standing next to the centers of attention), this could be just the hobby for you.

FINAL THOUGHTS

As we have navigated our way through America, it has become apparent that this vast, beautiful country shares some similarities between states but also some very unique and creative pastimes.

Hopefully, this sampling of hobbies from the various states has provided you with enough encouragement and that motivating factor for you to try something new and to get creative when determining your next activity, craft or project. Remember, you may need to modify your new hobby to fit well in your local environment.

If you are someone that has not done a lot of traveling close to home, maybe reading about other states has sparked your interest in setting out on a road trip to experience some of these hobbies first-hand.

Or perhaps you are now interested in researching more hobbies in your local state. With your new discoveries, feel free to write to me and let me know what you've found so I can consider that hobby for a future book. You may reach me at ravina@ravinachandra.com, and I look forward to hearing from you.

FROM THE AUTHOR

Thank you so much for reading *101 Ways to Enjoy Retirement Across America*. Please don't forget to write a brief review wherever you purchased this book. I am grateful for all feedback and your review will help other readers decide whether to read this book too. Follow this link to leave a review:

Interested in staying in touch to hear about any of my future books or projects? Would you like the opportunity to work with me directly in a personalized 90-day coaching program?

Contact me at ravina@ravinachandra.com

or visit www.ravinachandra.com

INDEX

Acting as an Extra, California, Chapter 43
Amateur Lapidary, Arkansas, Chapter 15
Amateur Racing, Indiana, Chapter 25
American Sign Language, Connecticut, Chapter 1
Antique Restoration, New Hampshire, Chapter 4
Architecture Appreciation, Iowa, Chapter 26

Beekeeping, Nebraska, Chapter 31
Bell Ringing, Massachusetts, Chapter 3
Blacksmithing, West Virginia, Chapter 23
Book-Binding, Colorado, Chapter 37
Butterfly Breeding, Georgia, Chapter 17

Card Games, Nevada, Chapter 47
Carnivorous Plants, South Carolina, Chapter 21
Cheesemaking, Wisconsin, Chapter 35
Clam Digging, Rhode Island, Chapter 5
Coding, *see Learning to Code*
Coin Shooting, Arizona, Chapter 36
Collecting Vinyl, Michigan, Chapter 28
Country Music, Tennessee, Chapter 22
Cryptograms, New Jersey, Chapter 9

Digital Libraries, Washington, Chapter 49
Disc Golf, Montana, Chapter 46
Dog Training, Alaska, Chapter 42
Drive-in Theatres, Florida, Chapter 16
Drone Photography, Montana, Chapter 46

Electric Bikes, Iowa, Chapter 26

Facial Hair Art, Wyoming, Chapter 50
Fantasy Sports, New York, Chapter 10
Farmers' Markets, Washington, Chapter 49
Feeding Hummingbirds, New Mexico, Chapter 38
Feeding Squirrels, North Carolina, Chapter 11
Fly Tying, Vermont, Chapter 6
Folk Music, Oklahoma, Chapter 39
Fountains, Missouri, Chapter 30
Fusion Cuisine, Louisiana, Chapter 19

Going Green, Idaho, Chapter 45
Graffiti, New Jersey, Chapter 9
Group Fitness, Florida, Chapter 16

Hamm Radio, Connecticut, Chapter 1
Hiking, Chapter 13, Virginia
Home-Brewing Kombucha, Oregon, Chapter 48
Hot Air Ballooning, Alabama, Chapter 14
Hula, Hawaii, Chapter 44

Ice Cream, *see Making Ice Cream*
Indoor Winter Sports, South Dakota, Chapter 34
Iris Folding, North Dakota, Chapter 32

Jazz Appreciation, Louisiana, Chapter 19

Kaleidoscopes, Oregon, Chapter 48
Kansas Style Barbecue, Kansas, Chapter 27

Laughing Clubs, Idaho, Chapter 45
Learning to Code, Delaware, Chapter 7
Leather Pyrography, Texas, Chapter 40

Letter Writing, Michigan, Chapter 28
Line-Dancing, Ohio, Chapter 33
Locksport, Massachusetts, Chapter 3

Macramé, Maine, Chapter 2
Magic Tricks, Nevada, Chapter 47
Mahjong, Maryland, Chapter 8
Making Ice Cream, New York, Chapter 10
Mazes and Meditation, Vermont, Chapter 6
Miniature Art, Pennsylvania, Chapter 12
Model Trains, Illinois, Chapter 24
Musical Theater, Oklahoma, Chapter 39

National Parks, Wyoming, Chapter 50
Natural Hot Springs or Sauna, Arkansas, Chapter 15
Natural Wonders, Alabama, Chapter 14
Nonviolent Hunting, Nebraska, Chapter 31

Online Learning, Arizona, Chapter 36

Paludariums, Maryland, Chapter 8
Pet Rocks, North Dakota, Chapter 32
Plane Spotting, Georgia, Chapter 17
Poetry Slams, California, Chapter 43
Potluck, Kansas, Chapter 27
Portraiture, South Dakota, Chapter 34
Pottery, Mississippi, Chapter 20

Quilting, North Carolina, Chapter 11

Riverboat Cruising, Mississippi, Chapter 20
RV Camping, Rhode Island, Chapter 5

Sand Art, South Carolina, Chapter 21

Self-Help, Ohio, Chapter 33
Short Stories, Maine, Chapter 2
Skipping Stones, Texas, Chapter 40
Snowshoeing, Alaska, Chapter 42
Social Media, Kentucky, Chapter 18
Song Writing, Kentucky, Chapter 18
Sport Shooting, Colorado, Chapter 37
Spotting UFOs, New Mexico, Chapter 38
Standup Paddle Boarding, Minnesota, Chapter 29
Stargazing, Utah, Chapter 41
Starting a Business, Delaware, Chapter 7
State Fairs, Minnesota, Chapter 29

Tablescaping, Missouri, Chapter 30
Tabletop Games, Utah, Chapter 41
Tarot Card Reading, Illinois, Chapter 24
Technology Free, Indiana, Chapter 25
Time Capsules, Pennsylvania, Chapter 12
Traveling the 'World', West Virginia, Chapter 23
Tree Shaping, Wisconsin, Chapter 35

Ukulele, Hawaii, Chapter 44

Vegetable Carving, New Hampshire, Chapter 4
Volunteering, Tennessee, Chapter 22

Wicca, Virginia, Chapter 13
Wedding Officiating, Washington, DC, Chapter 51

ENDNOTES

2. MAINE

1. https://www.thesprucecrafts.com/basic-macrame-knots-4176636

3. MASSACHUSETTS

1. https://people.csail.mit.edu/custo/MITLockGuide.pdf

4. NEW HAMPSHIRE

1. https://www.guinnessworldrecords.com/world-records/most-lit-jack-o-lanterns-displayed
2. Image by Mattes from Wikimedia Commons under Creative Commons Attribution-Share Alike 3.0 license.
3. Image by ศีลงูสาวสวยป่าแหวน from Wikimedia Commons under Creative Commons Attribution-Share Alike 3.0 license.

5. RHODE ISLAND

1. https://www.britannica.com/place/Rhode-Island-state
2. https://www.foodnetwork.com/recipes/anne-burrell/new-england-clam-chowder-recipe-1924845

6. VERMONT

1. Image from Wikimedia Commons under CC-Zero License.
2. Image from Wikipedia.com under CC BY-SA 3.0 license.

7. DELAWARE

1. https://insights.stackoverflow.com/survey/2020/

8. MARYLAND

1. Image by Kikkerdirk, from Getty Images under the Canvas Pro Creative Commons License.

10. NEW YORK

1. https://www.idfa.org/news-views/media-kits/ice-cream/the-history-of-ice-cream
2. https://www.pbs.org/food/the-history-kitchen/explore-the-delicious-history-of-ice-cream/

11. NORTH CAROLINA

1. Image by T Schofield from Getty Images, under Canva Pro Creative Common License.

12. PENNSYLVANIA

1. https://www.history.com/news/8-famous-time-capsules
2. Image by Cliffs, under the Creative Commons Attribution-Share Alike 4.0 International License

13. VIRGINIA

1. https://www.boston.com/news/local-news/2021/11/07/nimblewill-nomad-83-is-oldest-to-hike-appalachian-trail/
2. https://www.bergfreunde.eu/alpine-grades-calculator/
3. https://abcnews.go.com/WN/real-witches-practice-samhain-wicca-rise-us/story?id=8957950

14. ALABAMA

1. http://alabamajubilee.net/index.php
2. Image from Wikimedia commons, by Sheeba Samuel under the CC BY-SA 4.0 license.

17. GEORGIA

1. http://www.raisingbutterflies.org/getting_started
2. Image from Brande X Pictures under the Canvas Pro License.
3. https://en.wikipedia.org/wiki/List_of_the_busiest_airports_in_the_United_States

18. KENTUCKY

1. https://www.teneo.com, May 30th, 2020. The Most Socially Connected States Survey.
2. Adapted from: https://www.disciplemedia.com/building-your-community/positive-online-community/

19. LOUISIANA

1. https://www.hmart.com/recipe/post/chef-william-song-at-bopngrill-philly-bulkogi-eggroll/
2. https://www.mccormick.com/recipes/main-dishes/mexican-lasagna

22. TENNESSEE

1. https://bmcpublichealth.biomedcentral.com/articles/10.1186/s12889-017-4561-8
2. https://www.health.harvard.edu/blog/volunteering-may-be-good-for-body-and-mind-201306266428

26. IOWA

1. https://www.railstotrails.org/greatamericanrailtrail/

27. KANSAS

1. https://kansasfarmfoodconnection.org/recipes/bacon-cheeseburger-tater-tot-casserole

29. MINNESOTA

1. Image from Joe Shlabotnik (Flickr) under CC by 2.0 License

32. NORTH DAKOTA

1. From wikimedia commons, by June Campbell, under the Creative Commons Attribution-ShareAlike 3.0 License

33. OHIO

1. https://lithub.com/here-are-the-most-popular-self-help-books-in-every-state/

35. WISCONSIN

1. https://momsdish.com/recipe/267/farmers-cheese
2. https://cheesemaking.com/products/30-minute-mozzarella-recipe

40. TEXAS

1. Opera di Pirografia su legno di pioppo, by StefyMante, from WikimediaCommons under the Creative Commons Attribution-Share Alike 3.0 license.

41. UTAH

1. Image 'Stars 01' from Wikimedia Commons under Creative Commons Attribution-Share Alike 3.0 license

42. ALASKA

1. https://www.snowshoemag.com/wp-content/uploads/snowshoeing101.pdf

45. IDAHO

1. https://pocatello.us/462/US-Smile-Capital
2. https://www.ccpa-accp.ca/the-benefits-of-laughter

47. NEVADA

1. https://www.pagat.com/beating/mattis.html
2. https://www.masterclass.com/articles/learn-about-magic-tricks-and-6-tips-for-beginner-magicians

49. WASHINGTON

1. Image 'Pike Place Market' by Daniel Schwen from Wikimedia Commons under Creative Commons Attribution-ShareAlike 4.0 Generic License

50. WYOMING

1. https://www.worldbeardchampionships.com/

www.ingramcontent.com/pod-product-compliance
Lightning Source LLC
Chambersburg PA
CBHW031108080526
44587CB00011B/885